SKYE TERRIER

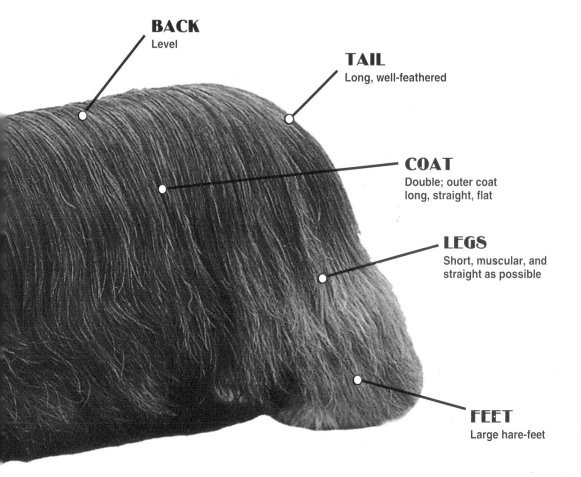

BACK
Level

TAIL
Long, well-feathered

COAT
Double; outer coat
long, straight, flat

LEGS
Short, muscular, and
straight as possible

FEET
Large hare-feet

Title page: Skye Terrier photographed by Paulette Braun.

Photographers: Ann Bower, Paulette Braun, Donald and Anne Brown, Rosemary Carroll, M. Connor, Laurie Erickson, Isabelle Francais, Robyn Hand, Sheri Kathol, Liane and Matthew Langbehn, M. Pesare, Vincent Serbin, Olga Smid, Judith Tabler

© T.F.H. Publications, Inc.

Distributed in the UNITED STATES to the Pet Trade by T.F.H. Publications, Inc., 1 TFH Plaza, Neptune City, NJ 07753; on the Internet at www.tfh.com; in CANADA by Rolf C. Hagen Inc., 3225 Sartelon St., Montreal, Quebec H4R 1E8; Pet Trade by H & L Pet Supplies Inc., 27 Kingston Crescent, Kitchener, Ontario N2B 2T6; in ENGLAND by T.F.H. Publications, PO Box 74, Havant PO9 5TT; in AUSTRALIA AND THE SOUTH PACIFIC by T.F.H. (Australia), Pty. Ltd., Box 149, Brookvale 2100 N.S.W., Australia; in NEW ZEALAND by Brooklands Aquarium Ltd., 5 McGiven Drive, New Plymouth, RD1 New Zealand; in SOUTH AFRICA by Rolf C. Hagen S.A. (PTY.) LTD., P.O. Box 201199, Durban North 4016, South Africa; in JAPAN by T.F.H. Publications. Published by T.F.H. Publications, Inc.

MANUFACTURED IN THE
UNITED STATES OF AMERICA
BY T.F.H. PUBLICATIONS, INC.

SKYE TERRIER

A COMPLETE AND RELIABLE HANDBOOK

Judith A. Tabler

RX-146

CONTENTS

INTRODUCTION

THE STORY OF GREYFRIARS BOBBY

Anyone interested in Skye Terriers should know the story of Greyfriars Bobby. Bobby was a young drop-eared Skye Terrier that was owned by a little girl who lived on a farm outside of Edinburgh, Scotland in 1858. However, Bobby decided that his master was an elderly man, Jock Gray, who worked on the farm. Once a week, on market day, Jock and Bobby traveled many miles into Edinburgh. The pattern of each market day was the same. Jock conducted his business until the one o'clock gun fired from Edinburgh Castle. That was the signal for Jock and Bobby to go for lunch at Mr. Traill's restaurant in Greyfriars.

Unfortunately, Jock soon became too old and sick to work on the farm, so he moved to Edinburgh. Bobby refused to have any other master but Jock. He ran away from the farm and eventually found Jock in the city. When Jock died, he was buried in Greyfriars Church-yard. Poor Bobby was heartbroken. Dogs were forbidden in the churchyard, but the determined Bobby crept in and began his 14-year vigil at Jock Gray's grave. Despite several serious attempts to move him, Bobby remained steadfast. He would have no home but the churchyard. He made his own daily schedule. At the one o'clock gun, Bobby ran into Mr. Traill's restaurant where he was greeted with a warm lunch.

The dog's faithfulness became legendary, and stories about him appeared in newspapers. People gathered at lunchtime to see Bobby come and go. His fame soon became a problem. Everyone in town knew the Skye Terrier's story, and Edinburgh had strict rules about stray dogs and dog licences. Bobby had no owner and no license, and eventually he had to appear in court. The Lord Provost of Edinburgh decided that Bobby's behavior had earned him "the keys to the city" and an "honorary" license. When Bobby died in 1872, he was buried near Jock Gray. Bobby's grave is marked by a headstone inscribed, "Let his loyalty and devotion be a lesson to us all." Baroness Burdett-Coutts was so touched by Bobby's story that she had a memorial fountain set up outside the churchyard. A life-sized statue of Bobby sits atop the fountain that supplies fresh drinking water on two levels—one for humans and one for canines. Bobby's story was poignantly told in 1961, when Walt Disney made the movie, *Greyfriars Bobby*, based on the book by Eleanor Atkinson.

If you are thinking about living with a Skye Terrier, remember Greyfriars Bobby. His story is not simply one of devotion between a dog and a man, but also a cautionary tale. Bobby had a will of his own. Ignoring the child who owned him, Bobby selected his own master. After his master's death, Bobby evaded all the well-meant attempts to house him. He decided where and how he would live. Bobby was a typical Skye Terrier.

"You may well believe any extravagant tale you may hear of the fidelity and affection of the Skye terrier...he's a well-knit little rascal, long and low, hardy and strong. His ancestors were bred for bolting foxes and wildcats among the rocky headlands of the subarctic islands. The intelligence, courage and devotion of dogs of this breed can scarcely be overstated. There is some far-away crossing here that gives this one (breed) a greater beauty and grace and more engaging manners, making him a 'sport' among rough farm dogs—but look at the length and strength of his muzzle. He's as determined as the deil (devil). You would have to break his neck before you could break his purpose. For love of his master he would starve, or he would leap to his death without an instant's hesitation."
from *Greyfriars Bobby*, page 238
by Eleanor Atkinson
Harper & Brothers, New York, 1912

Opposite: The poignant tale of Greyfriars Bobby, the faithful Skye Terrier made famous for his 14-year vigil at his master's gravesite, is legendary in Scotland. This life-sized statue of Bobby was erected in 1872 as a tribute to his loyalty. Photo courtesy of Sandra Goose Allen.

Greyfriars Bobby exemplified the typical Skye Terrier— an intelligent, courageous, and devoted companion. Photo courtesy of Sandra Goose Allen.

HISTORY OF THE SKYE TERRIER

The Skye Terrier is an ancient breed from the west coast of the Scottish Highlands. The region was first settled by the Picts from Ireland and later invaded by the Vikings, both of whom may have domesticated dogs. For centuries, men have used dogs to rid their houses and farms of vermin such as rats, mice, fox, otters, and badgers. By the middle of the 15th century, English writers started using the word "terrier" to describe any dog that dug down in the earth ("*terra*" in Latin) in pursuit of furred quarry. In the 16th century, Dr. John Caius, physician to King Edward VI, Queen Mary I, and Queen Elizabeth I, retired from his courtly duties and became Master of Gonville and Caius College at Cambridge in 1559. Caius took a keen interest in the variety of dogs in England and he catalogued them in his book entitled *Of English Dogges,* published in 1570. Because Scotland was an independent country, Caius does not include Scottish dogs, except for a reference to one long-coated Island dog from the barbarous north.

"Use and costume hath intertained other doggs of an outlandish kind, but a few and the same beyng of a pretty bygnesse, I mean Iseland, dogges curled and rough al over, which by reason of the length of their heare make showe neither of face nor of body. And yet these curres, forsoothe, because they are so straunge are greatly set by, esteemed, taken up, and made of many times in the rooms of the Spaniell gentle or comforter. The natures of men is so moved,

Opposite: The Skye Terrier is an ancient breed from the west coast of the Scottish Highlands. He is differentiated from other terriers by his long hair.

nay rather married to novelties without all reason wyt, judgement or perseverance.

Outlandish toyes we take with delight

Things of our owne notion we have in despight.

Which fault remainteh not in us concerning dogges only, but for artificers also, And why? it is to manyfest that wee disdayne and comtempne our own workmen, be they never so skillful, be they never so cunning, be they never so excellent. A beggerly beast brought out of the barbarous borders, fro' the uttermost countryes Northward, &c., we stare at, we glare at, we muse, we marvaile at, like an asse of Cumanum, like Thales with brasen shancks, like the man in the Moone." (p.37)

Because the Skye Terrier is differentiated from the other terrier breeds by his long hair, the passage about the "length of their heare make showe neither of face nor of body" is often cited as the earliest mention of a Skye Terrier. However, Caius also described the hair as "curled," an adjective that would not fit the breed today.

Another long-held theory traces the origin of the Skye Terrier to the defeat of the Spanish Armada in July of 1588. After the battle, the English sailors forced the retreating Spanish ships north and around the top of the isle of Britain. The Spanish fleet then turned south toward Spain, but storms wrecked many ships on the western coastal areas of Ireland and Scotland. The speculation is that among the shipwreck survivors were the Spanish sailors' dogs—long-haired Spaniels or Maltese types. These long-coated seafaring dogs then interbred with the local terriers and produced the ancestors of the current Skye Terriers. We have no way of knowing if the Spanish sailors had dogs on board, but the bones of a "whippet-like" dog were discovered on board the *Mary Rose*, an English warship that sank in 1545.

Another 16th-century story about the Skye Terrier should probably be included in the breed's history. In 1568, the Catholic Queen of Scots, Mary, was forced to abdicate her throne to her son. Mary fled to England where her cousin, Queen Elizabeth I, had her imprisoned. Sometime during the imprisonment, Mary is supposed to have acquired a Skye Terrier. In 1586,

The popularity of the Skye Terrier soared when Queen Victoria obtained the first of several Skyes in 1842. Woodcut by William Nicholson, courtesy of Mrs. J. S. W. Spofford.

H.M.The Queen.

Mary was found guilty of encouraging her followers to assassinate Elizabeth and the English Queen signed Mary's death warrant. Mary, Queen of Scots, was beheaded on February 8, 1587, at Fotheringay Castle. When the guards went to remove the body, they discovered the Skye Terrier hiding in her skirts. Covered in the Queen's blood, the Skye refused to move and began to howl. Elizabeth's ministers were already worried that any of Mary's remains would become sacred relics for her Catholic followers, so they had ordered all the Queen's clothing burned and the place of execution thoroughly scrubbed. Several of the guards finally captured the Skye and bathed him. The little dog would not be consoled, however, and he refused to eat. Queen Elizabeth was said to be enraged at the dog's devotion and gave orders to make him eat. But Skyes are not ruled by a Queen's dictates. The legend is that the little dog continued to pine for his mistress and soon died.

The evolution of the Skye Terrier breed does not become much clearer in the 17th and 18th centuries. In the writings about dogs from the period, most authors used the terms "Scottish" or "Scotch" to describe almost any terrier found in Scotland. One of the first clear references is in H. D. Richardson's *Dogs* in 1847. "The Skye Terrier, so called from its being found in the greatest perfection in the Western Isles of Scotland, and the Isle of Skye in particular." However, Skyes continued to be exhibited at dog shows as "Scotch Terriers" until 1861, when the Manchester Dog Show initiated the first separate class for the Skye.

The popularity of Skye Terriers soared when Queen Victoria obtained the first of several Skyes in 1842. Paintings of the royal family by Sir Edwin Landseer and the woodcut of the Queen by William Nicholson included charming Skyes. The Skye Terrier became the faddish pet of the social set. By the late 1890s, "a duchess would almost be ashamed to be seen in the park unaccompanied by her long-coated Skye."

Popularity changed the appearance of the breed. The small vermin-chasing Skye became a larger, more elegant dog with a profuse long coat. Some research indicates that Spaniels might have been interbred with Skyes to improve the quality of the coat. Ironically, these same changes probably diminished the popularity of the breed. By the end of the 19th century, most Skyes were too large to scramble down into holes after rodents and their coats required too much care. Farmers replaced their Skyes with other terrier breeds. Society people deserted the breed and moved on to another faddish dog long before the death of Queen Victoria in 1901.

Twentieth-century Skye Terriers have never enjoyed the limelight of their ancestors, but celebrity status rarely serves any dog breed well. True lovers of Skye Terriers have contently watched as the breed quietly slipped in the popularity polls. These devotees were no longer just English and Scottish. Skye Terriers were going international.

THE TWENTIETH CENTURY

For the past century, Skye Terriers have been a presence at most dog shows throughout Great Britain. Approximately 200 Skye puppies are registered each year. Thirty-eight Skyes were exhibited at the Crufts dog show in 1998. Unfortunately, no Skye Terrier has won Best in Show at Crufts since a Best in Show was first declared; however, Best Terrier wins have occurred twice. In 1907, a Skye called Wee Mac of Adel owned by Sir Claude Alexander won Best

Terrier. In 1974, the Best Terrier was a Skye called Ch. Silhill Silver Secret, owned by Mrs. S. Atkinson.

Some of the best 20th-century English and Scottish Skyes left their homeland to become foundation dogs for kennels throughout the world. Although European dog-breeding programs suffered greatly during the two World Wars, dog fanciers have persevered. Today, active breeders of Skye Terriers can be found in France, Germany, Austria, Switzerland, Italy, Sweden, Finland, Poland, Australia, New Zealand, South America, Canada, and the United States.

The first Skye Terrier registered by the American Kennel Club (AKC) was Romach in 1884. The breed has usually been represented at all large dog shows since that time. The founding of the Skye Terrier Club of America (STCA) was key to the preservation and to the improvement of the breed. Since its inception in 1938, the members of the STCA have devoted their time and energies to shepherding the Skye breed. Club members welcome and encourage anyone seeking information and advice about Skyes to contact them. They can be reached through the American Kennel Club in New York City (212-696-8200 or http://www.akc.org). From the AKC website, you can access all sorts of information about dogs, including terriers and Skyes, or you can go directly to the STCA home page (http://www.akc.org/clubs/skye) where you will find informative material on Skyes, along with telephone numbers and e-mail addresses of STCA members.

By the end of the 19th century, the appearance of the breed changed. The Skye Terrier became a larger, more elegant dog, with a profuse, long coat. Ch. Gillie Glass. Photo courtesy of Sandra Goose Allen.

Since the 1940s, the number of Skyes in the United States has remained fairly consistent. Between 100 and 150 Skye Terrier puppies are registered annually with the American Kennel Club. There was a burst of enthusiasm for the breed in the 1960s following the release of the Walt Disney movie, *Greyfriars Bobby*, and registration approached 400. Attention was also given to the breed in 1969 when Ch. Glamoor Good News became the only Skye Terrier to win the Best in Show at Westminster. In 1996, a beautiful black Skye, Ch. Finnsky Oliver from Finland, won the Terrier Group at Westminster. For the past 25 years, the registration number has hovered around 125. In 1997, 137 Skye puppies were registered. In 1998 there were 111 Skyes registered with The Kennel Club and 75 entries for the breed at Crufts in 1999.

Breeders of Skye Terriers are not dismayed by the breed's lack of popularity. Quite the opposite—conscientious dog breeders shudder when public attention focuses on a breed. Recently, Dalmatians have suffered with the attention brought to the breed by Walt Disney's *101 Dalmatians*. Both adults and children want that adorable puppy they saw in the movie, but few are ready for the care and responsibility that comes with a real-life animal. No animal should ever be an impulse purchase. Puppies purchased on impulse often end up neglected, bounced from home to home, or in animal shelters. Skye Terrier fanciers much prefer to see Skyes of great quality rather than a great quantity of Skyes.

Some of best 20th-century English and Scottish Skyes left their homeland to become foundation dogs for kennels throughout the world. Ch. Candlewyck Devil's Advocate, owned by Robyn Hand.

DESCRIPTION OF THE SKYE TERRIER

The Skye Terrier is an achrondroplastic or dwarf breed. A dwarf breed is a small dog, but small in a different way than a Toy breed. The term "dwarf" means that the proportions of the dog are atypical or distorted. A Toy dog is a miniature—a smaller version that remains in proportion. The Skye Terrier has bones and substance of a much larger dog. People who have seen photographs of Skyes are astounded when they have the opportunity to run their hands over a real dog. The large head and jaw, the long body, and the large strong bone structure are well-disguised under all that hair.

The Skye Terrier is a small dog, with a long, muscular body, short legs, and a large head. Ch. Roblyn Roadshow and Roblyn Lowrider, owned by Ann Boucher.

DESCRIPTION

The adjectives long, low, and lank are used repeatedly to describe the Skye Terrier's body shape. The Skye's exterior is directly related to the function for which it was bred. Farmers on the Isle of Skye, part of the Inner Hebrides off the northwest coast of Scotland, wanted a dog to hunt vermin. The Isle of Skye is almost as far north as Alaska and, although the ocean waters make the climate more temperate, the winter nights are long and the summer season is short. The weather is often cloudy and damp. The Cuillin Mountains are so often hidden in clouds that the Skye is nicknamed the "Misty Isle." The island's geography varies from mountain to moor to rocky coast. It is a perfect environment for a dog with a double coat.

The Skye Terrier was bred to do a job. Its assignment was to rid the island farms of destructive vermin. Such a dog needed a quick wit, a keen nose, and good eyesight to follow his prey to its hiding place. The dog needed short, strong legs with large feet and tough nails to dig down into the den. The quarry probably included mice, rats, foxes, otters, and badgers. Some of these animals are truly formidable fighters, especially underground in their own dens. To win in a battle to the death, the dog needed to be a fearless fighter with a large jaw, big teeth, and a muscular body. It took almost 400 years to perfect such a dog. But in the end, the Skye Terrier evolved to be just the right thing—a big dog on short legs.

Opposite: Although disguised under all that hair, the Skye Terrier has the bones and substance of a much larger dog.

The Skye's body type is directly related to the function for which he was bred: hunting.
His low body, short, strong legs, and keen senses enable him to dig down into the earth in pursuit of quarry hiding in its den.

STANDARD FOR THE SKYE TERRIER

In order to maintain quality, dog breeders agree on a standard for the breed. The dog described in the Skye Terrier Standard is the ideal Skye Terrier. Recognizing that the perfect dog specimen is always unattainable, breeders aim to breed dogs that have as few faults as possible. Dog shows are meant to encourage the improvement, because judges award top prizes to dogs that are closest to the standard for their breed. If you want to understand any breed of dog, you should become familiar with its standard. Contact the kennel club in your area for details on breed clubs, breeders, and the breed standard in your country.

AMERICAN KENNEL CLUB STANDARD
General Appearance—The Skye Terrier is a dog of

A dog of style, elegance, and dignity, the Skye Terrier is agile and strong, with sturdy bone and hard muscle. Am/Fin. Ch. Barraglen's Bobby Burns, owned by Donald and Anne Brown.

Int. Ch. Barraglen's Buccaneer demonstrates the breed's perfect proportions. His body is long, low, and level—the Skye is twice as long as he is high.

style, elegance and dignity: agile and strong with sturdy bone and hard muscle. Long, low and level—he is twice as long as he is high—he is covered with a profuse coat that falls straight down either side of the body over oval-shaped ribs. The hair well feathered on the head veils forehead and eyes to serve as protection from brush and briar as well as amid serious encounters with other animals. He stands with head high and long tail hanging and moves with a seemingly effortless gait. He is strong in body, quarter and jaw.

Size, Proportion, Substance—Size—The ideal shoulder height for dogs is 10 inches and 9 $\frac{1}{2}$ inches. Based on these heights a 10 inch dog measured from chest bone over tail at rump should be 20 inches. A slightly higher or lower dog of either sex is acceptable. Dogs 9 inches or less and bitches 8$\frac{1}{2}$ inches or less at the withers are to be penalized. ***Proportion***—The ideal ratio of body length to shoulder height is 2 to 1, which is considered the correct proportion. ***Substance***—Solidly built, full of strength and quality without being coarse. Bone is substantial.

Head—Long and powerful, strength being deemed more important than extreme length.

Eyes brown, preferably dark brown, medium in size, close-set and alight with life and intelligence. ***Ears*** symmetrical and gracefully feathered. They may be carried prick or drop. If prick, they are medium in size, placed high on the skull, erect at their outer edges, and slightly wider apart at the peak than at the skull. Drop ears, somewhat larger in size and set lower, hang flat against the skull.

Moderate width at the back of the skull tapers gradually to a strong muzzle. The stop is slight. The dark muzzle is just moderately full as opposed to snipy. Powerful and absolutely true jaws. The nose is always black. A Dudley, flesh-colored or brown nose shall disqualify. Mouth with the incisor teeth closing level, or with upper teeth slightly overlapping the lower.

Neck, Topline, Body—*Neck*—The neck is long and gracefully arched, carried high and proudly.

The backline is level.

Body is pre-eminently long and low, the chest deep, with oval-shaped ribs. The sides appear flattish due to the straight falling and profuse coat.

Tail is long and well feathered. When hanging, its upper section is pendulous, following the line of the rump, its lower section thrown back in a moderate arc without twist or curl. When raised, its height makes it appear a prolongation of the backline. Though not to be preferred, the tail is sometimes carried high when the dog is excited or angry. When such carriage arises from emotion only, it is permissible. But the tail should not be constantly carried above the level of the back or hang limp.

According to the standard, the Skye Terrier's long, straight double coat must be one overall color at the skin, but may be of varying shades of the same color in the full coat.

The Skye is friendly and loving with those he knows and cautious and reserved with strangers.

Forequarters—Shoulders well laid back, with tight placement of shoulder blades at the withers and elbows should fit closely to the sides and be neither loose nor tied. Forearm should curve slightly around the chest. Legs short, muscular and straight as possible. "Straight as possible" means straight as soundness and chest will permit, it does not mean "Terrier straight."

Feet—Large hare-feet preferably pointing forward, the pads thick and nails strong and preferably black.

Hindquarters—Strong, full, well developed and well angulated. Legs short, muscular and straight when viewed from behind. Feet as in front.

Coat—Double. Undercoat short, close, soft and woolly. Outer coat hard, straight and flat. 5 1/2 inches long without extra credit granted for greater length. The body coat hangs straight down each side, parting from head to tail. The head hair, which may be shorter, veils forehead and eyes and forms a moderate beard and apron. The long feathering on the ears falls straight down from the tips and outer edges, surrounding the ears like a fringe and outlining their shape. The ends of the hair should mingle with the coat of the neck. Tail well feathered.

Color—The coat must be of one over-all color at the skin but may be of varying shades of the same color in the full coat, which may be black, blue, dark or light grey, silver platinum, fawn or cream. The dog must have no distinctive markings except for the desirable black points of ears, muzzle and tip of tail, all of which points are preferably dark even to black. The shade of head and legs should approximate that of the body. There must be no trace of pattern, design or clear-cut color variations, with the exception of the breed's only permissible white which occasionally exists on the chest not exceeding 2 inches in diameter.

The puppy coat may be very different in color from the adult coat. Therefore, as it is growing and clearing, wide variations of color may occur; consequently, this is permissible in dogs under 18 months of age. However, even in puppies there must be no trace of pattern, design, or clear-cut variations with the exception of the black band encircling the body coat of the creme colored dog, and the only permissible white which, as in the adult dog, occasionally exists on the chest not exceeding 2 inches in diameter.

Gait—The legs proceed straight forward when traveling. When approaching, the forelegs form a continuation of the straight line of the front. The feet being the same distance apart as the elbows. The principal propelling power is furnished by the back legs which travel straight forward.

Forelegs should move well forward, without too much lift. The whole movement may be termed free, active and effortless and give a more or less fluid picture.

Temperament—The temperament is that of the typical working terrier capable of overtaking game and going to ground, displaying stamina, courage, strength and agility. Fearless, good-tempered, loyal and canny. The Skye is friendly and gay with those he knows and reserved and cautious with strangers.

DISQUALIFICATION

A Dudley, flesh-colored or brown nose shall disqualify.

Approved February 10, 1990
Effective March 28, 1990

ADDITIONAL COMMENTS

Most of the Skyes we see in the 20th century have erect, prick ears. One hundred years ago, the most common type of Skye was one with drop ears. Greyfriars Bobby was a drop-eared Skye and so were many belonging to Queen Victoria. The prick ears first appeared sometime in the late 19th century. In the early 1900s, there were so many Skyes of both types in the United Kingdom that dog show classes were divided and separate prizes awarded. Breeders attempted to keep the two strains pure, but following World War I the number of Skye Terriers dwindled. In order to maintain healthy bloodlines, the breeders resorted to crossing the best prick-eared dogs with the best drop-eared dogs. The result is that the drop ear continues to show up as a recessive gene.

Now, both varieties of ear carriage can be seen at large dog shows. While the prick-ears dominate the breed numerically, more and more drop ears are showing up. Once again, there are suggestions that the two varieties of ear sets be separated in breeding programs. Some breeders feel that continuing to mix the two strains weakens the erect prick ears and encourages poorly set drop ears. Floppy prick ears and poorly set drop ears are clearly penalized in the dog show ring. One breeder of show-quality Skyes told me, "Skye Terrier puppies come with three types of ear-sets: prick ears, drop ears, and heartbreak ears."

While erect prick ears dominate the breed, the Skye's ears may be carried prick or drop. Clan Donan the Black Douglas and Clan Donan the Highland Chief, owned by Donald and Anne Brown.

THE SKYE TERRIER TEMPERAMENT

The Skye Terrier is not a breed for everyone. Personally, I do not recommend them to someone who has never had a dog. Many of us make mistakes with our first dog, and the Skye is not a breed that

The Skye Terrier is not a breed recommended to someone who has never owned a dog. An intelligent and independent thinker, the Skye can be stubborn and needs a master who is in charge and can maintain that position with a firm, consistent attitude.

Smart and able, Skyes perform well as tracking, obedience, and agility dogs. Lairdogen Steel Magnolia NA exhibits the skills that made him the first Skye to receive an agility degree. Owner, Laura Weber.

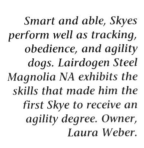

tolerates too many errors. They do not suffer fools gladly. Skyes are intelligent, independent thinkers, and they generally have their own opinion on how things should be done. Their masters need to exhibit calm confidence and consistency in order to gain the dog's respect. A Skye will quickly learn to disregard inconsistent and inexplicit commands, as well as the person who issues them.

It is important to establish early who is in charge and to maintain that position with a firm attitude. A Skye does not respond well to physical punishment. Such abuse can set up "terrier-like" defenses that may never be overcome. At the same time, most Skyes are exceedingly sensitive; a low stern voice, a firm "No," and a serious demeanor will usually get their attention.

The STCA emphasizes that the Skye is a "thinking breed." Too true. They have been selectively bred to outwit vermin. A Skye will challenge you mentally. They are smart and able when it suits their purposes, but they can be stubborn. It is not a good idea to "butt heads" over an issue—neither dog nor trainer benefits. The trick to training a Skye is to convince him that he wants to do something. This, again, is an area in which someone who is familiar with dogs benefits. Some dogs are motivated by an upbeat voice, others just by being with you, and still others need that special food for a reward. Skyes can and do perform well as tracking, obedience, and agility dogs—but their trainers have learned more than the dogs!

SELECTING A SKYE TERRIER

Where do you find a Skye Terrier? Call the American Kennel Club (AKC) in New York City (212 696-8200) or visit their website at http://www.akc.org. You also can go directly to the STCA home page (http://www.akc.org/clubs/skye). First, look at the information about rescue dogs at the STCA page or go directly to the Skye Rescue Foundation web site at http://www.geocities.com/Heartland/Valley/3533/skyeresq.htlm. In the UK, contact the Skye Terrier Breed Club or the Kennel Club for information on breeders in your area.

A rescue dog? The Skye people are as devoted to their dogs as they are to them. They have established a wonderful network to rescue Skye Terriers and to find them good homes. Most Skye Terriers are rescued from

There are many places you can look for a canine companion—check with the national breed club or a local rescue group. This is Edgar, a rescue dog that now lives with Anne Fresia and her cat.

homes where people do not understand how to socialize the dog or they give up on the coat care. They can be puppies or adults. Sometimes puppies or adults are abandoned, or it may be as simple as someone in the family became allergic to dogs. When the Skye Rescue people learn about a Skye that needs help, a member finds out all they can about the dog or puppy. The Skye is checked out medically and spayed or neutered. The dog then goes to live in a Skye foster home. The "foster person" evaluates the dog and makes recommendations as to the kind of family with which the dog will do best—with children, without children, with other dogs, or as a solo pet. A rescued Skye is the only kind that comes with handy, "easy-to-follow" directions and lots of future assistance from his Skye foster family.

Do you want a puppy or an adult? How much time do you have? The younger the puppy, the more time he demands. Is anyone home during the day? Someone has to take a puppy out several times during the day. A Skye matures slowly and does not reach adulthood until around 18 months to two years of age. Even an adult dog cannot be expected to stay inside through long workdays. And while a puppy may have a temperament that is more easily molded, you have to be around to mold it correctly.

Male or female? Males are usually slightly larger and heavier. An adult male Skye will weigh around 30 pounds, while females are closer to 25 pounds. Unless you or the breeder think that the puppy is destined for the show ring, you will probably spay or neuter the dog. Most dog breeders and veterinarians currently agree that these procedures are in the best interest for the health of a dog. The other consideration about the sex of a new dog might be if you already have a dog. Some older dogs are more welcoming if the new arrival is of the opposite sex.

Do you have a color preference? Skyes come in a wide range of colors, but it can be hard to tell exactly what color a puppy will become as he matures. Most Skyes are born black. They can stay black or change into blue, dark or light gray, silver platinum, fawn, or cream, all having darker markings on the nose and ears. Creams usually have a black line down the back while they are puppies. Light grays can turn silver or a creamy color that lightens into gray, and darker grays often start out as brindle. Irregular colors that are considered faults are a parti-color, usually black

As soon as your Skye is old enough, take him with you wherever you go. Introducing him to new people, places, and experiences will ensure that your dog is confident and well socialized.

with cream legs and cream under the tail, or brown, which will also have a brown nose.

SOCIALIZATION

This is a topic that could be included under temperament, but I believe it is sufficiently important enough to be discussed separately. The most important factor in raising a nice Skye Terrier is socialization. The more positive social experiences you can give your Skye, the nicer a dog you will have. I stress the word "positive" because of the incredible Skye memory. A slap on the nose from you or from the delivery person will not be quickly forgotten—or quickly forgiven.

Socialization does not come easily for many Skyes. The 400 years of breeding has aimed to make them "reserved and cautious with strangers," as it says in their breed standard. This trait makes them great watchdogs, but not always the best of company for guests. The best way to overcome this trait is to expose your puppy or dog to lots of nice people and places. When meeting people (including children), Skyes prefer to approach them. Even then, tell the person to talk to the dog and to let the dog smell the person's hands first. It may be the fall of hair hindering their vision, but many dogs recoil if anyone rushes at their heads. Some Skyes are never really comfortable being hugged or fondled by new acquaintances (including children) until they "take these

Opposite: An adult dog may be just the answer for people who do not have the patience or time to spend housebreaking or training a puppy.

31

people into their family." Fine with me—I like a dog that knows to whom he belongs.

LIVING WITH A SKYE

After our Chow died, we decided to get another dog. We no longer had small children and I was beginning to work at home. My family and I had been showing dogs for over 30 years and I knew something about most breeds. My breed had been Cocker Spaniels and we still had an older, gentle Cocker bitch. My husband had grown up with a Chow, but now he was willing to try a different breed. We agreed that we both like long-coated breeds, but my husband wanted a big dog, and I wanted a small dog.

I had known a neighbor's Skye when I was a child and always felt that he acted like a big dog. I began to watch the breed at dog shows and started talking to breeders. I was lucky to hear of a puppy quickly; often breeders have waiting lists. I visited the breeder at his home and met the puppies and their parents. A puppy's first teacher is his mother, so I like to meet the dam. I also want to see the puppy's early environment. These puppies were not off away from people. They were trotting around the yard and in and out of the kitchen and sitting room. They nonchalantly wandered around other adult dogs and came over to inspect me. The puppies were three months old and two bitches had been sold. I could pick from the three males. Each was equally

Before deciding to bring your Skye Terrier home, it is important to do your homework and learn as much as you can about the breed.

Dog ownership is a long-term commitment, so be sure your lifestyle will permit you to fulfill your Skye Terrier's needs for exercise, training, and companionship.

outgoing and adorable. Finally, (I swear) one picked me, so I picked him.

While I write this sentence, that same male Skye is asleep under my desk. His registered name is Ch. Cragsmoor For the Good, but he thinks it's "Troon." Troon was tan with black points (like a Siamese cat) when he first arrived at three months of age. The black points gradually turned gray, and the tan became first cream, and now, at age six, platinum. He likes to sleep with his back just touching my foot. He sleeps lightly, ready to move if he thinks the casters on my chair are creeping too close to his long hair. Always the watchdog, he points toward the door and will race downstairs if someone approaches the house. By the way, our stairs are not steep; steep stairs and lots of them can be hard on Skyes with their long torso and short legs.

Troon has the deep bark of a large dog and uses it frequently when someone approaches the house. I do not discourage this. I want a watchdog, and a firm "Quiet, that's enough" will stop his barking. Troon likes people. He is pleased to see visitors and delighted when it is someone he knows. But he backs off warily if someone he does not know begins to hug him. Brae, our three-year-old, dark gray bitch, reacts to company in a more reserved fashion. I always know when my college-age son has friends downstairs. Brae politely wags and welcomes them. She is happy to be patted, but then she leaves to find me. She will then sit by me until those big, noisy boys leave. I have yet to figure out if she is protecting me, or I am protecting her.

Despite the fall of hair in their eyes, Troon and Brae spend a great deal of time watching things. Both are fascinated by Winston (the neighbors' Springer Spaniel), squirrels, birds, and the occasional duck. Troon also watches television. He is partial to videos of himself, but also likes nature shows with lots of animal sounds—elk mating calls are his favorites. The dogs love to swim in the local pond, but neither is too keen on the saltwater waves at the beach. Other Skye owners tell me that I just did not introduce the beach correctly and that their dogs delight in romps in the surf. One Skye named Angus is fond of sailing and sports his lifevest proudly.

Roxy, our Cocker Spaniel, likes the summertime, but Troon and Brae are not fond of hot weather. During the hottest days, they find spots for naps near air conditioners. Each August, I begin to worry that the Skyes have slowed down with age. Then comes the first cold snap and they are rejuvenated. Puppy-like, they play tag. Troon is always "it" and he chases Brae around the bushes and through the fall leaves. Two Skyes are great fun, because they do play together. Troon tried and tried to get Roxy to play, but she rarely engaged. The two Skyes are on the same wavelength. They understand each other's body language and really enjoy games together. Brae can be a bit bossy, but Troon seems to ignore it.

When it snows, they are even wilder. Both dogs love to run in it. Then they stretch out to have long, back-scratching rolls in the white stuff. Troon is quite happy to sit in the snow for ages—I can't actually say how long he would sit there, because I always make him come in before he wants to. (Coming in is never a problem by the way, because the dogs are *always* rewarded with a treat when they come.)

Troon is a good eater, but Brae used to be finicky. She has learned that the dishes are removed after a decent amount of time has passed—about 15 minutes. I feed the dogs in separate rooms so that Troon does not have the chance to clean up Brae's leftovers.

The dogs know about when my husband comes home and station themselves next to the door. They are always rewarded with a walk, followed by dog biscuits in their beds. Our dinner preparation usually goes smoothly, but occasionally it has been interrupted by a plush squeaky toy landing up on the counter. Skyes will shake a toy so hard that it flies up and away. They usually stay around the table during dinner. Troon will jump into a seemingly uncomfortable Windsor chair and watch us eat. He seems to want to be on the same level. None of the dogs are given "people food," so they never beg for any. If it is a real doggy sort of night, my husband might indulge them in a sing-along. The dogs know the word "Sing!" and put back their heads to howl like hounds. Brae actually has more of a yelp, but Troon has a wonderful deep "baritone." Troon never sings on the floor; he always sits in a chair.

Troon understands 25 to 35 words and other phrases. His wonderful prick ears perk up to attention, and he cocks his head at the mention of his name or to listen to a conversation of interest. I love the way he uses his ears to listen, and I was given advice on how to encourage it when he was a puppy. I was told to talk to him and make lots of funny noises when I was around him. His favorite words are "School" and "Muffin." School is obedience class, which he loves to attend, and Muffin is my mother's Bichon Frise. Muffin and Troon were puppies together. He just about somersaults at the sound of her name.

Our dogs have a last walk and then go to their beds—not ours. They love to get up on our bed, but sleeping there at night has never been an option. They have all joined me for naps when I had the flu, but no one resists the nighttime arrangements. When each was a puppy, they slept in a crate. I still use crates for any kind of travel, and I crate my dogs when things are too confusing around the house. For example, they are crated when

First-time dog owners should consider signing up for obedience classes. An experienced trainer can teach you how to establish household rules and how to prevent problem behaviors from occurring, like jumping up on the furniture.

workmen are here for any length of time. Workmen can leave tools and chemicals around, and I don't want any dog wandering out an untended door. Brae is happy to be crated, but Troon "grumbles" on the way in and refuses to eat any treat given to him while crated. But, if I am not using the crate and Troon just happens to be by the open door, he will often go in for a nap. Typical Skye!

TRAINING TIPS

A crate is one of the best training tools you will ever purchase. Buy one that is long enough for your puppy or dog to stretch out comfortably—24" x 20" x 20" is the minimum. Teach your Skye about the crate gradually. Let the puppy see that it is a good place to eat, play with a favorite toy, and hear lots of praise. Once the puppy is accustomed to the crate, close the door for a few minutes. If the pup fusses, wait until he is quiet and then let him out. Most puppies settle down and take to their crates as a wild animal might to his den. However, don't leave a puppy or dog in a pen for longer than three or four hours. They need to go out!

Skyes are basically a clean breed and easy to house-break. The crate is the key to housebreaking. Skyes do not like to soil their "dens." As soon as you take your puppy out of his crate, take him outside. Do this as soon as the pup wakes up in the morning, about a half hour after he eats (the younger the pup, the more often he eats), several additional times during the day, and just before he goes to bed for the night. While it is important to give the puppy plenty of access to water, some people like to limit the amount given during the night. Praise your puppy or dog lavishly when he does his business where you want him to, but remember that a puppy cannot really control his urine or feces until he is five or six months of age. Even later mistakes will occur, and the only time to scold your Skye is when you catch him in the act and tell him, "No." I use a firm tone and say, "No, Outside," and we go outside together. Skyes should not be too hard to housebreak. They like to keep their crates clean and this clean space gradually extends to more and more area. The biggest pitfall is in not getting the puppy outside often enough so that he has to mess in the crate. You do not want to allow the dog to become used to having a dirty crate.

When training your dog to a collar leash, use a soft buckle collar for a young puppy and a rolled leather collar for an adult. I do not leave my collars on my dogs in the house, but many people do. Check the collar often to make sure it is not too tight or rubbing off too much coat. I use a light leash with a young dog, but I use a strong narrow leather lead on a full-grown Skye. They are low-set dogs, not weak ones. Leash training usually progresses smoothly as long as you use the Skye's natural curiosity (and sometimes special food treats) to motivate him, and give him a lot of praise and encouragement when he goes where you want him to go and firm and gentle discipline when you disagree. Remember to avoid those "head-butting" confrontations, because no one wins. Terriers have been bred to stubbornly "hold on." We even use the adjective "terrier-like" to describe such behavior.

I take my dogs to "dog school." We go to puppy socialization classes first. The dogs exhibit much enthusiasm about going, and I learn a lot about training the dog. Some "dog schools" offer to take the dog and train him for you. I would not do this with my Skye. Skyes have a tendency to be one man or woman dogs and I want the dog to respect me—not someone else. I also think it is important to understand my Skye from shared experiences, not just have someone else tell me about it. Training a Skye can be an intellectually challenging experience. The best Skye trainers are so "tuned in" to their dogs that they anticipate problems and work on ways around them.

Crate training is the easiest and fastest way to housetrain your Skye. Crates can also be used to keep your pet safe during travel.

YOUR PUPPY'S NEW HOME

Before actually collecting your puppy, it is better that you purchase the basic items you will need in advance of the pup's arrival date. This allows you more opportunity to shop around and ensure you have exactly what you want rather than having to buy lesser quality in a hurry.

It is always better to collect the puppy as early in the day as possible. In most instances this will mean that the puppy has a few hours with your family before it is time to retire for his first night's sleep away from his former home.

If the breeder is local, then you may not need any form of box to place the puppy in when you bring him

These adorable 10-week-old Skye puppies are ready to go their new homes. Before collecting your pup, be sure to purchase the basic items he'll need and have a supply of the food he's been eating on hand.

To keep your curious Skye pup from harm, be sure to puppy-proof your home and leave him in a safe fenced-in play area when he's outdoors.

home. A member of the family can hold the pup in his lap—duly protected by some towels just in case the puppy becomes car sick! Be sure to advise the breeder at what time you hope to arrive for the puppy, as this will obviously influence the feeding of the pup that morning or afternoon. If you arrive early in the day, then they will likely only give the pup a light breakfast so as to reduce the risk of travel sickness.

If the trip will be of a few hours duration, you should take a travel crate with you. The crate will provide your pup with a safe place to lie down and rest during the trip. During the trip, the puppy will no doubt wish to relieve his bowels, so you will have to make a few stops. On a long journey you may need a rest yourself, and can take the opportunity to let the puppy get some fresh air. However, do not let the puppy walk where there may have been a lot of other dogs because he might pick up an infection. Also, if he relieves his bowels at such a time, do not just leave the feces where they were dropped. This is the height of irresponsibility. It has resulted in many public parks and other places actually banning dogs. You can purchase poop-scoops from your pet shop and should have them with you whenever you are taking the dog out where he might foul a public place.

Your journey home should be made as quickly as possible. If it is a hot day, be sure the car interior is amply supplied with fresh air. It should never be too hot or too cold for the puppy. The pup must never be placed where he might be subject to a draft. If the journey requires an overnight stop at a motel, be aware that other guests will not appreciate a puppy crying half the night. You must regard the puppy as a baby and comfort him so he does not cry for long periods. The worst thing you can do is to shout at or smack him. This will mean your relationship is off to a really bad start. You wouldn't smack a baby, and your puppy is still very much just this.

ON ARRIVING HOME

By the time you arrive home the puppy may be very tired, in which case he should be taken to his

Opposite: Although it's tempting, do not introduce your Skye puppy to friends and neighbors for at least 48 hours, especially if he's not fully vaccinated. He needs time to adjust to his new environment and to build up his immunities.

It is important that you know how to hold a fragile puppy the proper way. To lift a pup, place your right hand under his chest, use your left hand to hold his neck, and then bring him close to your chest.

sleeping area and allowed to rest. Children should not be allowed to interfere with the pup when he is sleeping. If the pup is not tired, he can be allowed to investigate his new home—but always under your close supervision. After a short look around, the puppy will no doubt appreciate a light meal and a drink of water. Do not overfeed him at his first meal because he will be in an excited state and more likely to be sick.

Although it is an obvious temptation, you should not invite friends and neighbors around to see the new arrival until he has had at least 48 hours in which to settle down. Indeed, if you can delay this longer then do so, especially if the puppy is not fully vaccinated. At the very least, the visitors might introduce some local bacteria on their clothing that the puppy is not immune to. This aspect is always a risk when a pup has been moved some distance, so the fewer people the pup meets in the first week or so the better.

DANGERS IN THE HOME

Your home holds many potential dangers for a little mischievous puppy, so you must think about these in advance and be sure he is protected from them. The more obvious are as follows:

Open Fires. All open fires should be protected by a mesh screen guard so there is no danger of the pup being burned by spitting pieces of coal or wood.

Electrical Wires. Puppies just love chewing on things, so be sure that all electrical appliances are neatly hidden from view and are not left plugged in when not in use. It is not sufficient simply to turn the plug switch to the off position—pull the plug from the socket.

Open Doors. A door would seem a pretty innocuous object, yet with a strong draft it could kill or injure a puppy easily if it is slammed shut. Always ensure there is no risk of this happening. It is most likely during warm weather when you have windows or outside doors open and a sudden gust of wind blows through.

Balconies. If you live in a high-rise building, obviously the pup must be protected from falling. Be sure he cannot get through any railings on your patio, balcony, or deck.

Ponds and Pools. A garden pond or a swimming pool is a very dangerous place for a little puppy to be near. Be sure it is well screened so there is no risk of

Ask your breeder to supply you with a cloth or toy that has been with your Skye's mother or littermates. The familiar smell will be comforting to your puppy when placed in his new sleeping area.

the pup falling in. It takes barely a minute for a pup—or a child—to drown.

The Kitchen. While many puppies will be kept in the kitchen, at least while they are toddlers and not able to control their bowel movements, this is a room full of danger—especially while you are cooking. When cooking, keep the puppy in a play pen or in another room where he is safely out of harm's way. Alternatively, if you have a carry box or crate, put him in this so he can still see you but is well protected.

Be aware, when using washing machines, that more than one puppy has clambered in and decided to have a nap and received a wash instead! If you leave the washing machine door open and leave the room for any reason, then be sure to check inside the machine before you close the door and switch on.

Small Children. Toddlers and small children should never be left unsupervised with puppies. In spite of such advice it is amazing just how many people not only do this but also allow children to pull and maul pups. They should be taught from the outset that a puppy is not a plaything to be dragged about the home—and they should be promptly scolded if they disobey.

Children must be shown how to lift a puppy so it is safe. Failure by you to correctly educate your children about dogs could one day result in their getting a very nasty bite or scratch. When a puppy is lifted, his weight must always be supported. To lift the pup, first place your right hand under his chest. Next, secure the pup by using your left hand to hold his neck. Now

43

you can lift him and bring him close to your chest. Never lift a pup by his ears and, while he can be lifted by the scruff of his neck where the fur is loose, there is no reason ever to do this, so don't.

Beyond the dangers already cited you may be able to think of other ones that are specific to your home—steep basement steps or the like. Go around your home and check out all potential problems—you'll be glad you did.

THE FIRST NIGHT

The first few nights a puppy spends away from his mother and littermates are quite traumatic for him. He will feel very lonely, maybe cold, and will certainly miss the heartbeat of his siblings when sleeping. To help overcome his loneliness it may help to place a clock next to his bed—one with a loud tick. This will in some way soothe him, as the clock ticks to a rhythm not dissimilar from a heart beat. A cuddly toy may also help in the first few weeks. A dim nightlight may provide some comfort to the puppy, because his eyes will not yet be fully able to see in the dark. The puppy may want to leave his bed for a drink or to relieve himself.

If the pup does whimper in the night, there are two things you should not do. One is to get up and chastise him, because he will not understand why you are shouting at him; and the other is to rush to comfort him

The first few weeks in a new home may be difficult for a young puppy. Providing your Skye with a warm bed and some cuddly toys can help him feel safe and secure. Five-month-old Olivia Magig of Skyelove settles in for a cozy nap.

If you have other pets in the home, your new puppy should be introduced to them under careful supervision.

every time he cries because he will quickly realize that if he wants you to come running all he needs to do is to holler loud enough!

By all means give your puppy some extra attention on his first night, but after this quickly refrain from so doing. The pup will cry for a while but then settle down and go to sleep. Some pups are, of course, worse than others in this respect, so you must use balanced judgment in the matter. Many owners take their pups to bed with them, and there is certainly nothing wrong with this.

The pup will be no trouble in such cases. However, you should only do this if you intend to let this be a permanent arrangement, otherwise it is hardly fair to the puppy. If you have decided to have two puppies, then they will keep each other company and you will have few problems.

OTHER PETS

If you have other pets in the home then the puppy must be introduced to them under careful supervision. Puppies will get on just fine with any other pets—but you must make due allowance for the respective sizes of the pets concerned, and appreciate that your puppy has a rather playful nature. It would be very foolish to leave him with a young rabbit. The pup will want to play and might bite the bunny and get altogether too rough with it. Kittens are more able to

45

defend themselves from overly cheeky pups, who will get a quick scratch if they overstep the mark. The adult cat could obviously give the pup a very bad scratch, though generally cats will jump clear of pups and watch them from a suitable vantage point. Eventually they will meet at ground level where the cat will quickly hiss and box a puppy's ears. The pup will soon learn to respect an adult cat; thereafter they will probably develop into great friends as the pup matures into an adult dog.

Opposite: As your Skye grows up, he will need care, kindness, and encouragement to become a well-adjusted adult.

HOUSETRAINING

Undoubtedly, the first form of training your puppy will undergo is in respect to his toilet habits. To achieve this you can use either newspaper, or a large litter tray filled with soil or lined with newspaper. A puppy cannot control his bowels until he is a few months old, and not fully until he is an adult. Therefore you must anticipate his needs and be prepared for a few accidents. The prime times a pup will urinate and defecate are shortly after he wakes up from a sleep, shortly after he has eaten, and after he has been playing awhile. He will usually whimper and start searching the room for a suitable place. You must quickly pick him up and place him on the newspaper or in the litter tray. Hold him in position gently but firmly. He might jump out of the box without doing anything on the first one or two occasions, but if you simply repeat the procedure every time you think he wants to relieve himself then eventually he will get the message.

When he does defecate as required, give him plenty of praise, telling him what a good puppy he is. The litter tray or newspaper must, of course, be cleaned or replaced after each use—puppies do not like using a dirty toilet any more than you do. The pup's toilet can be placed near the kitchen door and as he gets older the tray can be placed outside while the door is open. The pup will then start to use it while he is outside. From that time on, it is easy to get the pup to use a given area of the yard.

Many breeders recommend the popular alternative of crate training. Upon bringing the pup home, introduce him to his crate. The open wire crate is the best choice, placed in a restricted, draft-free area of the home. Put the pup's Nylabone® and other favorite toys in the crate along with a wool blanket or other suitable bedding. The puppy's natural cleanliness instincts prohibit him from soiling in the place where

he sleeps, his crate. The puppy should be allowed to go in and out of the open crate during the day, but he should sleep in the crate at the night and at other intervals during the day. Whenever the pup is taken out of his crate, he should be brought outside (or to his newspapers) to do his business. Never use the crate as a place of punishment. You will see how quickly your pup takes to his crate, considering it as his own safe haven from the big world around him.

Opposite: Because Skye Terriers bond strongly with everyone in the family, your companionship is necessary to their happiness and well-being.

THE EARLY DAYS

You will no doubt be given much advice on how to bring up your puppy. This will come from dog-owning friends, neighbors, and through articles and books you may read on the subject. Some of the advice will be sound, some will be nothing short of rubbish. What you should do above all else is to keep an open mind and let common sense prevail over prejudice and worn-out ideas that have been handed down over the centuries. There is no one way that is superior to all others, no more than there is no one dog that is exactly a replica of another. Each is an individual and must always be regarded as such.

A dog never becomes disobedient, unruly, or a menace to society without the full consent of his owner. Your puppy may have many limitations, but the singular biggest limitation he is confronted with in so many instances is his owner's inability to understand his needs and how to cope with them.

IDENTIFICATION

It is a sad reflection on our society that the number of dogs and cats stolen every year runs into many thousands. To these can be added the number that get lost. If you do not want your cherished pet to be lost or stolen, then you should see that he is carrying a permanent identification number, as well as a temporary tag on his collar.

Permanent markings come in the form of tattoos placed either inside the pup's ear flap, or on the inner side of a pup's upper rear leg. The number given is then recorded with one of the national registration companies. Research laboratories will not purchase dogs carrying numbers as they realize these are clearly someone's pet, and not abandoned animals. As a result, thieves will normally abandon dogs so marked and this at least gives the dog a chance to be taken to the police or the dog pound, when the number

can be traced and the dog reunited with its family. The only problem with this method at this time is that there are a number of registration bodies, so it is not always apparent which one the dog is registered with (as you provide the actual number). However, each registration body is aware of his competitors and will normally be happy to supply their addresses. Those holding the dog can check out which one you are with. It is not a perfect system, but until such is developed it's the best available.

Another permanent form of identification is the microchip, a computer chip that is no bigger than a grain of rice that is injected between the dog's shoulder blades. The dog feels no discomfort. The dog also receives a tag that says he is microchipped. If the dog is lost and picked up by the humane society, they can trace the owner by scanning the microchip. It is the safest form of identification.

A temporary tag takes the form of a metal or plastic disk large enough for you to place the dog's name and your phone number on it—maybe even your address as well. In virtually all places you will be required to obtain a license for your puppy. This may not become applicable until the pup is six months old, but it might apply regardless of his age. Much depends upon the state within a country, or the country itself, so check with your veterinarian if the breeder has not already advised you on this.

Make sure you take your Skye outside to relieve himself after every meal. Remember to use positive reinforcement and praise, which are important parts of the housebreaking process.

FEEDING YOUR SKYE TERRIER

For the first few weeks of life, a baby Skye Terrier's mother is his key to survival and his source of food, warmth, and security. Ch. Rikaabah's Bashful Bianca and baby Limbo's Eloise del Barril, owned by Susy de Umana.

Dog owners today are fortunate in that they live in an age when considerable cash has been invested in the study of canine nutritional requirements. This means dog food manufacturers are very concerned about ensuring that their foods are of the best quality. The result of all of their studies, apart from the food itself, is that dog owners are bombarded with advertisements telling them why they must purchase a given brand. The number of products available to you is unlimited, so it is hardly surprising to find that dogs in general suffer from

obesity and an excess of vitamins, rather than the reverse. Be sure to feed age-appropriate food—puppy food up to one year of age, adult food thereafter. Generally breeders recommend dry food supplemented by canned, if needed.

FACTORS AFFECTING NUTRITIONAL NEEDS

Activity Level. A dog that lives in a country environment and is able to exercise for long periods of the day will need more food than the same breed of dog living in an apartment and given little exercise.

Quality of the Food. Obviously the quality of food will affect the quantity required by a puppy. If the nutritional content of a food is low then the puppy will need more of it than if a better quality food was fed.

Balance of Nutrients and Vitamins. Feeding a puppy the correct balance of nutrients is not easy because the average person is not able to measure out ratios of one to another, so it is a case of trying to see that nothing is in excess. However, only tests, or your veterinarian, can be the source of reliable advice.

Genetic and Biological Variation. Apart from all of the other considerations, it should be remembered that each puppy is an individual. His genetic make-up will influence not only his physical characteristics but also his metabolic efficiency. This being so, two pups from the same litter can vary quite a bit in the amount of food they need to perform the same function under the same conditions. If you consider the potential combinations of all of these factors then you will see that pups of a given breed could vary quite a bit in the amount of food they will need. Before discussing feeding quantities it is valuable to know at least a little about the composition of food and its role in the body.

Opposite: Your Skye Terrier should have a healthy, well-balanced diet that includes the proper amount of proteins, fats, and carbohydrates.

COMPOSITION AND ROLE OF FOOD

The main ingredients of food are protein, fats, and carbohydrates, each of which is needed in relatively large quantities when compared to the other needs of vitamins and minerals. The other vital ingredient of food is, of course, water. Although all foods obviously contain some of the basic ingredients needed for an animal to survive,

they do not all contain the ingredients in the needed ratios or type. For example, there are many forms of protein, just as there are many types of carbohydrates. Both of these compounds are found in meat and in vegetable matter—but not all of those that are needed will be in one particular meat or vegetable. Plants, especially, do not contain certain amino acids that are required for the synthesis of certain proteins needed by dogs.

Likewise, vitamins are found in meats and vegetable matter, but vegetables are a richer source of most. Meat contains very little carbohydrates. Some vitamins can be synthesized by the dog, so do not need to be supplied via the food. Dogs are carnivores and this means their digestive tract has evolved to need a high quantity of meat as compared to humans. The digestive system of carnivores is unable to break down the tough cellulose walls of plant matter, but it is easily able to assimilate proteins from meat.

In order to gain its needed vegetable matter in a form that it can cope with, the carnivore eats all of its prey. This includes the partly digested food within the stomach. In commercially prepared foods, the cellulose is broken down by cooking. During this process the vitamin content is either greatly reduced or lost

Always be sure to feed age-appropriate food designed to meet the nutritional needs of your puppy, adult, or senior dog. Am/Can. Ch. Roblyn A Chorus Line TDX, Can. TD, and four of her puppies, owned by Laura Weber.

altogether. The manufacturer therefore adds vitamins once the heat process has been completed. This is why commercial foods are so useful as part of a feeding regimen, providing they are of good quality and from a company that has prepared the foods very carefully.

Proteins

These are made from amino acids, of which at least ten are essential if a puppy is to maintain healthy growth. Proteins provide the building blocks for the puppy's body. The richest sources are meat, fish and poultry, together with their by-products. The latter will include milk, cheese, yogurt, fishmeal, and eggs. Vegetable matter that has a high protein content includes soy beans, together with numerous corn and other plant extracts that have been dehydrated. The actual protein content needed in the diet will be determined both by the activity level of the dog and his age. The total protein need will also be influenced by the digestibility factor of the food given.

Fats

These serve numerous roles in the puppy's body. They provide insulation against the cold, and help buffer the organs from knocks and general activity shocks. They provide the richest source of energy,

The amount of exercise your Skye receives affects his food intake. A very active dog will require more to eat than a less active dog of the same size. Ch. Cragsmoor For The Good and Cragsmoor A Good Finesse, owned by Judith Tabler.

and reserves of this, and they are vital in the transport of vitamins and other nutrients, via the blood, to all other organs. Finally, it is the fat content within a diet that gives it palatability. It is important that the fat content of a diet should not be excessive. This is because the high energy content of fats (more than twice that of protein or carbohydrate) will increase the overall energy content of the diet. The puppy will adjust its food intake to that of its energy needs, which are obviously more easily met in a high-energy diet. This will mean that while the fats are providing the energy needs of the puppy, the overall diet may not be providing its protein, vitamin, and mineral needs, so signs of protein deficiency will become apparent. Rich sources of fats are meat, their byproducts (butter, milk), and vegetable oils, such as safflower, olive, corn or soy bean.

Opposite: The best way to determine if your puppy's diet is sufficient is by checking his bone and muscle development, his weight, and his level of activity.

Carbohydrates

These are the principal energy compounds given to puppies and adult dogs. Their inclusion within most commercial brand dog foods is for cost, rather than dietary needs. These compounds are more commonly known as sugars, and they are seen in simple or complex compounds of carbon, hydrogen, and oxygen. One of the simple sugars is called glucose, and it is vital to many metabolic processes. When large chains of glucose are created, they form compound sugars. One of these is called glycogen, and it is found in the cells of animals. Another, called starch, is the material that is found in the cells of plants.

Vitamins

These are not foods as such but chemical compounds that assist in all aspects of an animal's life. They help in so many ways that to attempt to describe these effectively would require a chapter in itself. Fruits are a rich source of vitamins, as is the liver of most animals. Many vitamins are unstable and easily destroyed by light, heat, moisture, or rancidity. An excess of vitamins, especially A and D, has been proven to be very harmful. Provided a puppy is receiving a balanced diet, it is most unlikely there will be a deficiency, whereas hypervitaminosis (an excess of vitamins) has become quite common due to owners and breeders feeding unneeded supplements. The only time you should

feed extra vitamins to your puppy is if your veterinarian advises you to.

Minerals

These provide strength to bone and cell tissue, as well as assist in many metabolic processes. Examples are calcium, phosphorous, copper, iron, magnesium, selenium, potassium, zinc, and sodium. The recommended amounts of all minerals in the diet has not been fully established. Calcium and phosphorous are known to be important, especially to puppies. They help in forming strong bone. As with vitamins, a mineral deficiency is most unlikely in pups given a good and varied diet. Again, an excess can create problems—this applying equally to calcium.

Water

This is the most important of all nutrients, as is easily shown by the fact that the adult dog is made up of about 60 percent water, the puppy containing an even higher percentage. Dogs must retain a water balance, which means that the total intake should be balanced by the total output. The intake comes either by direct input (the tap or its equivalent), plus water released when food is oxidized, known as metabolic water (remember that all foods contain the elements hydrogen and oxygen that recombine in the body to create water). A dog without adequate water will lose condition more rapidly than one depleted of food, a fact common to most animal species.

AMOUNT TO FEED

The best way to determine dietary requirements is by observing the puppy's general health and physical appearance. If he is well covered with flesh, shows good bone development and muscle, and is an active alert puppy, then his diet is fine. A puppy will consume about twice as much as an adult (of the same breed). You should ask the breeder of your puppy to show you the amounts fed to their pups and this will be a good starting point.

The puppy should eat his meal in about five to seven minutes. Any leftover food can be discarded or placed into the refrigerator until the next meal (but be sure it is thawed fully if your fridge is very cold).

If the puppy quickly devours its meal and is clearly still hungry, then you are not giving him enough food. If he eats readily but then begins to pick at it, or walks away leaving a quantity, then you are probably giving him too much food. Adjust this at the next meal and you will quickly begin to appreciate what the correct amount is. If, over a number of weeks, the pup starts to look fat, then he is obviously overeating; the reverse is true if he starts to look thin compared with others of the same breed.

WHEN TO FEED

It really does not matter what times of the day the puppy is fed, as long as he receives the needed quantity of food. Puppies from 8 weeks to 12 or 16 weeks need 3 or 4 meals a day. Older puppies and adult dogs should be fed twice a day. What is most important is that the feeding times are reasonably regular. They can be tailored to fit in with your own timetable—for example, 7 a.m. and 6 p.m. The dog will then expect his meals at these times each day. Keeping regular feeding times and feeding set amounts will help you monitor your puppy's or dog's health. If a dog that's normally enthusiastic about mealtimes and eats readily suddenly shows a lack of interest in food, you'll know something's not right.

Establishing a feeding schedule with set amounts of food will help you to monitor your Skye's overall health.

GROOMING YOUR SKYE TERRIER

If you own a Skye, both you and the Skye should learn about grooming. This maxim is true whether your Skye is a show dog or a housepet. If you are dealing with a puppy, start the lessons early. Don't wait until the long hair has arrived.

Lesson one: Get the puppy used to lying on his side while you brush him gently with a pin brush. Use the word "Stay," and praise him for lying still. The weekly

A potential Skye Terrier owner should realize that the dog's long, double coat will require considerable grooming to keep it healthy and looking nice.

brushing should be a good chance to thoroughly go over the puppy. Stand the puppy squarely on his legs and tell him to stay. Check for any bumps or cuts. Also examine his ears, mouth, and feet. Very few Skyes have ear problems, but all dogs need regular teeth cleaning as adults. It is easy if the dog thinks this is part of his routine. Puppy nails should be clipped just below the quick with a dog nail trimmer. Do not take off too much, or the nails will hurt and bleed. (Most Skyes do not forget that.) The correct amount is not always easy to judge when the dog has black nails. If you are unsure just how far to trim, ask your veterinarian to show you. For a young puppy, the grooming sessions should be short and sweet. Relaxed puppy grooming sessions are the best route to easy adult grooming sessions.

Lesson two: Skyes mature at different speeds, but the puppy coat should begin to change around seven months of age. Increase your grooming sessions to help the puppy shed his old puppy hair and make way for his glorious double adult coat. Extra care during this transition phase will avoid a great deal of hard work later.

Lesson three: You then must deal with the adult coat. With your Skye on his side, take your pin brush and travel down the length of the hair with long smooth strokes. When you encounter a mat or snarl, work it loose with your fingers. Sometimes a little dusting of cornstarch on the hair can help with the untangling. Skyes seem to like to collect mats behind their ears and any place where one part of the body rubs against another, such as between the forelegs and the chest. However, an insect bite or scratch from a twig can cause a Skye to scratch and make a mat just about any place.

A couple of personal words of advice about these grooming sessions: 1) make them a weekly commitment so that there is never too much time for mats to build up; and 2) make them a time to enjoy being with your dog. I have several dogs (four Skyes and a Cocker Spaniel). All but one dog presents himself at grooming time, because I am completely devoted to that dog for about an hour. Also, keep it light. The dogs are much more relaxed if I greet each mat with an upbeat, "Whoops, what do we have here?" and some gentle finger unknotting rather than a disgusted "Oh, I don't believe it. Not another one!"

Lesson four: The bath, if needed. The bath should always come after the brush out; otherwise, you are knotting up those mats for good. A Skye only needs to be bathed once a week if he is competing in shows. Dirty hair breaks more easily than clean hair. If you are brushing your Skye regularly, you can keep the dog quite clean; however, you should know how to bathe him when the time comes. There are many good dog shampoos available, but the key to washing a Skye is to let the shampoo and the water flow through the coat. Do not rub the hair or you will tangle it. Rinse out the shampoo and follow the same procedure with a creme rinse. Make sure that all the shampoo and creme rinse are out; any residue can irritate the skin and cause itching.

Lesson five: Dry the dog. I use a hair dryer (the ones made for dogs work the best). Set the dryer on either medium or low heat (the hot setting is too hot for dogs—never use it). Using a pin brush and wide tooth comb and always moving with the natural direction of the hair, gently brush and comb the dog dry.

Lesson six: A perfectly groomed Skye has his hair parted straight down his back. Since you trained your Skye to stand in lesson one, tell him to stay. Locate his spine at the base of the tail. Begin the part there and move forward. I use a wide tooth comb, but some people use a knitting needle to separate the hair. Part it an inch at a time all the way up and over the ears. It is not as hard as it looks, because you follow right along the spine. My Skyes like to give a good shake as soon as I have finished. (This may be related to some ticklishness or to their sense of humor!) If you make the part often enough, the hair begins to fall into place naturally.

Keeping your pet well groomed is important to his health and well-being.

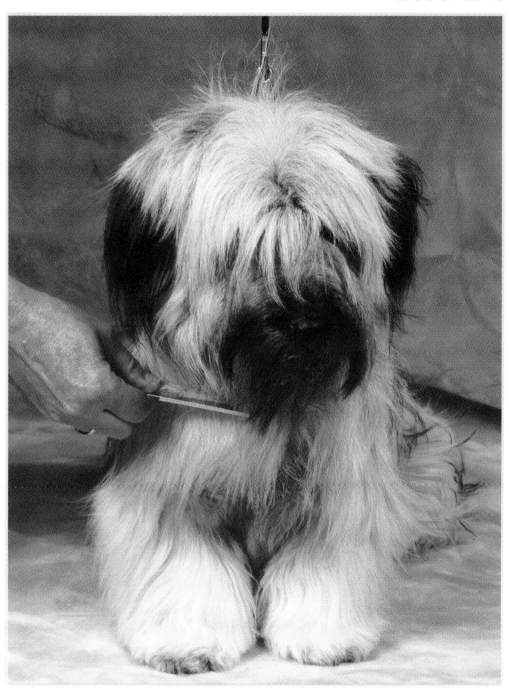

Begin grooming your dog at an early age—it will help him to become accustomed to the weekly procedure. This well-behaved Skye is comfortable being combed.

Lesson seven: Skye paws need just a little trimming. Feel between the pads for excessive or matted hair. These mats should be very carefully cut out with small blunt-nosed scissors. The long hair should be trimmed off the bottom of the pads. Look at your Skye's foot when he stands squarely on all fours. Any long, untidy hairs can be trimmed around the paws.

TRAINING YOUR SKYE TERRIER

Once your puppy has settled into your home and responds to his name, then you can begin his basic training. Before giving advice on how you should go about doing this, two important points should be made. You should train the puppy in isolation of any potential distractions, and you should keep all lessons very short. It is essential that you have the full attention of your puppy. This is not possible if there

Opposite: Do not allow your Skye off-leash until he reliably responds to your commands—for his safety and the safety of others.

You can begin basic training once your new puppy has settled into your home and responds to his name.

are other people about, or televisions and radios on, or other pets in the vicinity. Even when the pup has become a young adult, the maximum time you should allocate to a lesson is about 20 minutes. However, you can give the puppy more than one lesson a day, three being as many as are recommended, each well spaced apart.

Before beginning a lesson, always play a little game with the puppy so he is in an active state of mind and thus more receptive to the matter at hand. Like-wise, always end a lesson with fun-time for the pup, and always—this is most important—end on a high note, praising the puppy. Let the lesson end when the pup has done as you require so he receives lots of fuss. This will really build his confidence.

COLLAR AND LEASH TRAINING

Training a puppy to his collar and leash is very easy. Place a collar on the puppy and, although he will initially try to bite at it, he will soon forget it, the more so if you play with him. You can leave the collar on for a few hours. Some people leave their dogs' collars on all of the time, others only when they are taking the dog out. If it is to be left on, purchase a narrow or round one so it does not mark the fur.

Once the puppy ignores his collar, then you can attach the leash to it and let the puppy pull this along behind it for a few minutes. However, if the pup starts to chew at the leash, simply hold the leash but keep it slack and let the pup go where he wants. The idea is to let him get the feel of the leash, but not get in the habit of chewing it. Repeat this a couple of times a day for two days and the pup will get used to the leash without thinking that it will restrain him—which you will not have attempted to do yet.

Next, you can let the pup understand that the leash will restrict his movements. The first time he realizes this, he will pull and buck or just sit down. Immediately call the pup to you and give him lots of fuss. Never tug on the leash so the puppy is dragged along the floor, as this simply implants a negative thought in his mind.

THE COME COMMAND

Come is the most vital of all commands and espe-cially so for the independently minded dog. To teach the puppy to come, let him reach the end of a long lead, then give the command and his name, gently

The sit is the foundation command for everything else your dog will learn. Miss Midget, CD, CGC, TT, owned by Liane and Matthew Langbehn, performs the perfect sit/stay.

pulling him toward you at the same time. As soon as he associates the word come with the action of moving toward you, pull only when he does not respond immediately. As he starts to come, move back to make him learn that he must come from a distance as well as when he is close to you. Soon you may be able to practice without a leash, but if he is slow to come or notably disobedient, go to him and pull him toward you, repeating the command. Never scold a dog during this exercise—or any other exercise. Remember the trick is that the puppy must want to come to you. For the very independent dog, hand signals may work better than verbal commands.

THE SIT COMMAND

As with most basic commands, your puppy will learn this one in just a few lessons. You can give the puppy two lessons a day on the sit command but he will make just as much progress with one 15-minute lesson each day. Some trainers will advise you that you should not proceed to other commands until the previous one has been learned really well. However, a bright young pup is quite capable of handling more than one command per lesson, and certainly per day. Indeed, as time progresses, you will be going through each command as a matter of routine before a new one is attempted. This is so the puppy always starts, as well as ends, a lesson on a high note, having successfully completed something.

67

Call the puppy to you and fuss over him. Place one hand on his hindquarters and the other under his upper chest. Say "Sit" in a pleasant (never harsh) voice. At the same time, push down his rear end and push up under his chest. Now lavish praise on the puppy. Repeat this a few times and your pet will get the idea. Once the puppy is in the sit position you will release your hands. At first he will tend to get up, so immediately repeat the exercise. The lesson will end when the pup is in the sit position. When the puppy understands the command, and does it right away, you can slowly move backwards so that you are a few feet away from him. If he attempts to come to you, simply place him back in the original position and start again. Do not attempt to keep the pup in the sit position for too long. At this age, even a few seconds is a long while and you do not want him to get bored with lessons before he has even begun them.

Opposite: The heel exercise can teach your dog to walk beside you without pulling, which will make your daily outings together more enjoyable.

THE HEEL COMMAND

All dogs should be able to walk nicely on a leash without their owners being involved in a tug-of-war. The heel command will follow leash training. Heel training is best done where you have a wall to one side of you. This will restrict the puppy's lateral movements, so you only have to contend with forward and backward situations. A fence is an alternative, or you can do the lesson in the garage. Again, it is better to do the lesson in private, not on a public sidewalk where there will be many distractions.

With a puppy, there will be no need to use a choke collar as you can be just as effective with a regular one. The leash should be of good length, certainly not too short. You can adjust the space between you, the puppy, and the wall so your pet has only a small amount of room to move sideways. This being so, he will either hang back or pull ahead—the latter is the more desirable state as it indicates a bold pup who is not frightened of you.

Hold the leash in your right hand and pass it through your left. As the puppy moves ahead and strains on the leash, give the leash a quick jerk backwards with your left hand, at the same time saying "Heel." The position you want the pup to be in is such that his chest is level with, or just behind, an imaginary line from your knee. When the puppy is in this position, praise him and begin walking again, and the whole exercise will be

repeated. Once the puppy begins to get the message, you can use your left hand to pat the side of your knee so the pup is encouraged to keep close to your side.

It is useful to suddenly do an about-turn when the pup understands the basics. The puppy will now be behind you, so you can pat your knee and say "Heel." As soon as the pup is in the correct position, give him lots of praise. The puppy will now be beginning to associate certain words with certain actions. Whenever he is not in the heel position he will experience displeasure as you jerk the leash, but when he comes alongside you he will receive praise. Given these two options, he will always prefer the latter—assuming he has no other reason to fear you, which would then create a dilemma in his mind.

Once the lesson has been well learned, then you can adjust your pace from a slow walk to a quick one and the puppy will come to adjust. The slow walk is always the more difficult for most puppies, as they are usually anxious to be on the move.

If you have no wall to walk against then things will be a little more difficult because the pup will tend to wander to his left. This means you need to give lateral jerks as well as bring the pup to your side. End the lesson when the pup is walking nicely beside you. Begin the lesson with a few sit commands (which he understands by now), so you're starting with success and praise. If your puppy is nervous on the leash, you should never drag him to your side as you may see so many other people do (who obviously didn't invest in a good book like you did!). If the pup sits down, call him to your side and give lots of praise. The pup must always come to you because he wants to. If he is dragged to your side he will see you doing the dragging—a big negative. When he races ahead he does not see you jerk the leash, so all he knows is that something restricted his movement and, once he was in a given position, you gave him lots of praise. This is using canine psychology to your advantage.

Always try to remember that if a dog must be disciplined, then try not to let him associate the discipline with you. This is not possible in all matters but, where it is, this is definitely to be preferred.

THE STAY COMMAND

This command follows from the sit. Face the puppy and say "Sit." Now step backwards, and as you do, say "Stay." Let the pup remain in the position for only a few seconds before calling him to you and giving lots of praise. Repeat this, but step further back. You do not need to shout at the puppy. Your pet is not deaf; in fact, his hearing is far better than yours. Speak just loudly enough for the pup to hear, yet use a firm voice. You can stretch the word to form a "sta-a-a-y." If the pup gets up and comes to you simply lift him up, place him back in the original position, and start again. As the pup comes to understand the command, you can move further and further back.

The next test is to walk away after placing the pup. This will mean your back is to him, which will tempt him to follow you. Keep an eye over your shoulder, and the minute the pup starts to move, spin around and, using a sterner voice, say either "Sit" or "Stay." If the pup has gotten quite close to you, then, again, return him to the original position.

Aside from having practical uses, the stay command teaches your dog self-control. He should be able to remain in position until you release him, as this obedient Skye demonstrates with a down/stay.

As the weeks go by you can increase the length of time the pup is left in the stay position—but two to three minutes is quite long enough for a puppy. If your puppy drops into a lying position and is clearly more comfortable, there is nothing wrong with this. Likewise, your pup will want to face the direction in which you walked off. Some trainers will insist that the dog

faces the direction he was placed in, regardless of whether you move off on his blind side. I have never believed in this sort of obedience because it has no practical benefit.

THE DOWN COMMAND

From the puppy's viewpoint, the down command can be one of the more difficult ones to accept. This is because the position is one taken up by a submissive dog in a wild pack situation. A timid dog will roll over—a natural gesture of submission. A bolder pup will want to get up, and might back off, not feeling he should have to submit to this command. He will feel that he is under attack from you and about to be punished—which is what would be the position in his natural environment. Once he comes to understand this is not the case, he will accept this unnatural position without any problem.

You may notice that some dogs will sit very quickly, but will respond to the down command more slowly—it is their way of saying that they will obey the command, but under protest!

There two ways to teach this command. One is, in my mind, more intimidating than the other, but it is up to you to decide which one works best for you. The first method is to stand in front of your puppy and bring him to the sit position, with his collar and leash on. Pass the leash under your left foot so that when you pull on it, the result is that the pup's neck is forced downwards. With your free left hand, push the pup's shoulders down while at the same time saying "Down." This is when a bold pup will instantly try to back off and wriggle in full protest. Hold the pup firmly by the shoulders so he stays in the position for a second or two, then tell him what a good dog he is and give him lots of praise. Repeat this only a few times in a lesson because otherwise the puppy will get bored and upset over this command. End with an easy command that brings back the pup's confidence.

The second method, and the one I prefer, is done as follows: Stand in front of the pup and then tell him to sit. Now kneel down, which is immediately far less intimidating to the puppy than to have you towering above him. Take each of his front legs and pull them forward, at the same time saying "Down." Release the legs and quickly apply light pressure on the shoulders with your left hand. Then, as quickly, say "Good boy" and give lots of fuss. Repeat two or three times only.

The pup will learn over a few lessons. Remember, this is a very submissive act on the pup's behalf, so there is no need to rush matters.

RECALL TO HEEL COMMAND

When your puppy is coming to the heel position from an off-leash situation—such as if he has been running free—he should do this in the correct manner. He should pass behind you and take up his position and then sit. To teach this command, have the pup in front of you in the sit position with his collar and leash on. Hold the leash in your right hand. Give him the command to heel, and pat your left knee. As the pup starts to move forward, use your right hand to guide him behind you. If need be you can hold his collar and walk the dog around the back of you to the desired position. You will need to repeat this a few times until the dog understands what is wanted.

When he has done this a number of times, you can try it without the collar and leash. If the pup comes up toward your left side, then bring him to the sit position in front of you, hold his collar and walk him around the back of you. He will eventually understand and automatically pass around your back each time. If the dog is already behind you when you recall him, then he should automatically come to your left side, which you will be patting with your hand.

Be firm and consistent when teaching your Skye the no command. It could save his life someday and can help curb common behavior problems, like jumping up on your favorite chair.

The time invested in training will benefit both dog and owner for a lifetime. Ch. Barraglen's Brankie Birk, owned by Ann Bower.

THE NO COMMAND

This is a command that must be obeyed every time without fail. There are no halfway stages, he must be 100-percent reliable. Most delinquent dogs have never been taught this command; included in these are the jumpers, the barkers, and the biters. Were your puppy to approach a poisonous snake or any other potential danger, the no command, coupled with the recall, could save his life. You do not need to give a specific lesson for this command because it will crop up time and again in day-to-day life.

If the puppy is chewing a slipper, you should approach the pup, take hold of the slipper, and say "No" in a stern voice. If he jumps onto the furniture, lift him off and say "No" and place him gently on the floor. You must be consistent in the use of the command and apply it every time he is doing something you do not want him to do.

HEALTH CONCERNS OF THE SKYE TERRIER

The Skye Terrier is essentially a very healthy breed and has fewer medical problems than some other purebred dogs. While your dog's veterinarian is the best place to seek medical advice, you may want to know additional details about the breed and health. If so, consult the Skye Terrier Club of America (http://www.akc.org/clubs/skye), or in the UK, Skye Terrier Club, Mrs. M. Watts, Lilybank, Westfield, Ossett, West Yorkshire WF5 8JH, England, 01924 270386. Medically knowledgeable STCA members have formed a health committee to compile data pertinent to the health of the Skye. They have supplied the information below.

Skyes are not affected by hip dysplasia, PRA, and cardiomegaly. They do have problems that are breed specific and others that are common but not breed specific.

The breed-specific problems are:

(1) Premature closure of the distal radius. This is a condition in which one of the growth plates in the front leg(s) closes before the other one. This causes an abnormal elbow joint, limping as a puppy, and early arthritic changes as an adult. The cause of this problem is genetic as well as traumatic. Young Skye puppies (up to seven months of age) should have restrictions on some activity (no jumping on and off furniture, hard surfaces, stairs, etc.). If

limping occurs in a Skye puppy, a veterinarian should be consulted.

(2) Skye Hepatitis. This is a rare condition that occurs in young dogs (ages two to five) and is fatal. It is a genetic disease that results in liver failure and has no effective treatment. Symptoms are abdominal swelling, nausea, jaundice, and weight loss.

(3) Some Skyes have shown adverse reactions to Ivermectin™. Because there are so few Skyes, statistical data is not always well publicized. Most veterinarians are aware that Collies cannot tolerate Ivermectin™. Please tell your veterinarian that Skyes have a similar reaction. Treatment with

Although the Skye Terrier is essentially a very healthy breed and has fewer medical problems than some other purebred dogs, it's important to be aware of breed-specific health concerns.

Ivermectin™ should be avoided with Skyes. Ivermectin is found in some types of heartworm medication and can be used in treating conditions such as sarcoptic mange.

The problems that are not breed specific are:

(1) Breast Cancer. This is a problem in all unspayed females and is a very common problem in Skye Terriers. The STCA health committee has a research project with Michigan State University to identify the gene associated with breast cancer in Skyes (and possibly in all dogs).

(2) Autoimmune disease. This has been identified as the number-one problem in purebred dogs by the AKC, and this is a common problem in Skyes. It may show as hypothyroid disease, bleeding disorders, or gastrointestinal disorders. All these conditions are treatable and may not affect the longevity of the dog.

(3) Disc disease. This back problem, a "slipped disc," is not as common as one would think, considering the Skye's length of back and shortness of legs. Other dwarf breeds have a much higher occurrence rate than the Skye Terrier, but it does occur in older dogs. It usually requires surgery.

(4) Hemangiosarcoma. This is a tumor of the spleen that is very difficult to diagnose and may cause a dog distress due to a rupture of the tumor. This tumor is more common in other breeds, but it is becoming more common in Skye Terriers. Unfortunately, this tumor is difficult to treat and usually fatal.

While your veterinarian is the best source of advice, you can also check with the Skye Terrier Club of America. They compile up-to-date health information about the breed that you can access at their web site.

YOUR HEALTHY SKYE TERRIER

Dogs, like all other animals, are capable of contracting problems and diseases that, in most cases, are easily avoided by sound husbandry—meaning well-bred and well-cared-for animals are less prone to developing diseases and problems than are carelessly bred and neglected animals. Your knowledge of how to avoid problems is far more valuable than all of the books and advice on how to cure them. Respectively, the only person you should listen to about treatment is your vet. Veterinarians don't have all the answers, but at least they are trained to analyze and treat illnesses, and are aware of the full implications of treatments. This does not mean a few old remedies aren't good standbys when all else fails, but in most cases modern science provides the best treatments for disease.

PHYSICAL EXAMS

Your puppy should receive regular physical examinations or check-ups. These come in two forms. One is obviously performed by your vet, and the other is a day-to-day procedure that should be done by you. Apart from the fact the exam will highlight any problem at an early stage, it is an excellent way of socializing the pup to being handled.

To do the physical exam yourself, start at the head and work your way around the body. You are looking for any sign of lesions, or any indication of parasites on the pup. The most common parasites are fleas and ticks.

Opposite: As a responsible Skye Terrier owner, you should have a basic understanding of the medical problems that affect the breed.

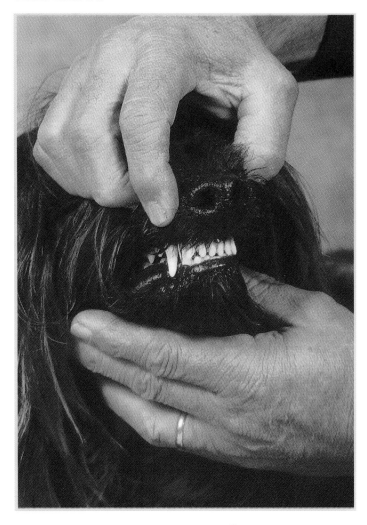

Healthy teeth and gums are important to the well-being of your Skye Terrier. Check and brush his teeth regularly.

HEALTHY TEETH AND GUMS

Chewing is instinctual. Puppies chew so that their teeth and jaws grow strong and healthy as they develop. As the permanent teeth begin to emerge, it is painful and annoying to the puppy, and puppy owners must recognize that their new charges need something safe upon which to chew. Unfortunately, once the puppy's permanent teeth have emerged and settled solidly into the jaw, the chewing instinct does not fade. Adult dogs instinctively need to clean their teeth, massage their gums, and exercise their jaws through chewing.

It is necessary for your dog to have clean teeth. You should take your dog to the veterinarian at least once a year to have his teeth cleaned and to have his mouth examined for any sign of oral disease. Although dogs do not get cavities in the same way humans do, dogs'

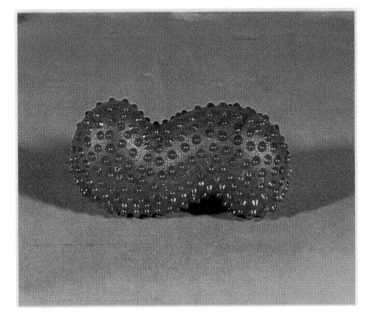

The Hercules® by Nylabone® has raised dental tips that help fight plaque on your Skye's teeth.

teeth accumulate tartar, and more quickly than humans do! Veterinarians recommend brushing your dog's teeth daily. But who can find time to brush their dog's teeth daily? The accumulation of tartar and plaque on our dog's teeth when not removed can cause irritation and eventually erode the enamel and finally destroy the teeth. Advanced cases, while destroying the teeth, bring on gingivitis and periodontitis, two very serious conditions that can affect the dog's internal organs as well...to say nothing about bad breath!

Raised dental tips on the surface of every Plaque Attacker™ help to combat plaque and tartar.

Since everyone can't brush their dog's teeth daily or get to the veterinarian often enough for him to scale

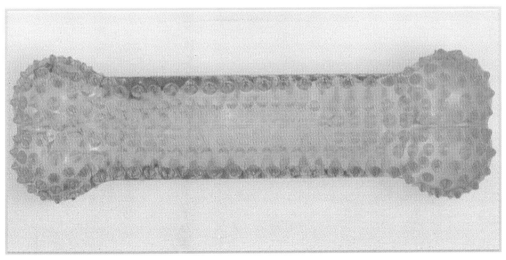

the dog's teeth, providing the dog with something safe to chew on will help maintain oral hygeine. Chew devices from Nylabone® keep dogs' teeth clean, but they also provide an excellent resource for entertainment and relief of doggie tensions. Nylabone® products give your dog something to do for an hour or two every day and during that hour or two, your dog will be taking an active part in keeping his teeth and gums healthy…without even realizing it! That's invaluable to your dog, and valuable to you!

Nylabone® provides fun bones, challenging bones, and *safe* bones. It is an owner's responsibility to recognize safe chew toys from dangerous ones. Your dog will chew and devour anything you give him. Dogs must not be permitted to chew on items that they can break. Pieces of broken objects can do internal damage to a dog, besides ripping the dog's mouth. Cheap plastic or rubber toys can cause stoppage in the intestines; such stoppages are operable only if caught immediately.

The most obvious choices, in this case, may be the worst choice. Natural beef bones were not designed for chewing and cannot take too much pressure from the sides. Due to the abrasive nature of these bones, they should be offered most sparingly. Knuckle bones, though once very popular for dogs, can be easily

Nylabone® is the only plastic dog bone made of 100 percent virgin nylon, specially processed to create a tough, durable, completely safe bone.

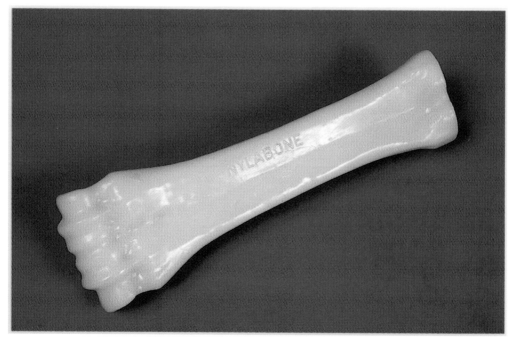

There are many dangers that your dog may encounter in the great outdoors, so closely supervise him when he is outside.

chewed up and eaten by dogs. At the very least, digestion is interrupted; at worst, the dog can choke or suffer from intestinal blockage.

When a dog chews hard on a Nylabone®, little bristle-like projections appear on the surface of the bone. These help to clean the dog's teeth and add to the gum-massaging. Given the chemistry of the nylon, the bristle can pass through the dog's intestinal tract without effect. Since nylon is inert, no microorganism can grow on it, and it can be washed in soap and water or sterilized in boiling water or in an autoclave.

For the sake of your dog, his teeth and your own peace of mind, provide your dog with Nylabones®. They have 100 variations from which to choose.

FIGHTING FLEAS

Fleas are very mobile and may be red, black, or brown in color. The adults suck the blood of the host, while the larvae feed on the feces of the adults, which is rich in blood. Flea "dirt" may be seen on the pup as very tiny clusters of blackish specks that look like freshly ground pepper. The eggs of fleas may be laid on the puppy, though they are more commonly laid off the host in a favorable place, such as the bedding. They normally hatch in 4 to 21 days, depending on the temperature, but they can survive for up to 18 months if temperature conditions are not favorable. The larvae are maggot-like and molt a couple of times before forming pupae, which can survive long periods until the temperature, or the vibration of a nearby host, causes them to emerge and jump on a host.

There are a number of effective treatments available, and you should discuss them with your veterinarian, then follow all instructions for the one you choose. Any treatment will involve a product for your puppy or dog and one for the environment, and will require diligence on your part to treat all areas and thoroughly clean your home and yard until the infestation is eradicated.

THE TROUBLE WITH TICKS

Ticks are arthropods of the spider family, which means they have eight legs (though the larvae have six). They bury their headparts into the host and gorge on its blood. They are easily seen as small grain-like creatures sticking out from the skin. They are often picked up when dogs play in fields, but may also arrive in your yard via wild animals—even birds—or stray cats and dogs. Some ticks are species-specific, others are more adaptable and will host on many species.

The cat flea is the most common flea of dogs. It starts feeding soon after it makes contact with the dog.

The deer tick is the most common carrier of Lyme disease. Photo courtesy of Virbac Laboratories, Inc., Fort Worth, Texas.

The most troublesome type of tick is the deer tick, which spreads the deadly Lyme disease that can cripple a dog (or a person). Deer ticks are tiny and very hard to detect. Often, by the time they're big enough to notice, they've been feeding on the dog for a few days—long enough to do their damage. Lyme disease was named for the area of the United States in which it was first detected—Lyme, Connecticut—but has now been diagnosed in almost all parts of the U.S. Your veterinarian can advise you of the danger to your dog(s) in your area, and may suggest your dog be vaccinated for Lyme. Always go over your dog with a fine-toothed flea comb when you come in from walking through any area that may harbor deer ticks, and if your dog is acting unusually sluggish or sore, seek veterinary advice.

Attempts to pull a tick free will invariably leave the headpart in the pup, where it will die and cause an infected wound or abscess. The best way to remove ticks is to dab a strong saline solution, iodine, or alcohol on them. This will numb them, causing them to loosen their hold, at which time they can be removed with forceps. The wound can then be cleaned and covered with an antiseptic ointment. If ticks are common in your area, consult with your vet for a suitable pesticide to be used in kennels, on bedding, and on the puppy or dog.

INSECTS AND OTHER OUTDOOR DANGERS

There are many biting insects, such as mosquitoes, that can cause discomfort to a puppy. Many diseases are transmitted by the males of these species.

A pup can easily get a grass seed or thorn lodged between his pads or in the folds of his ears. These may go unnoticed until an abscess forms.

This is where your daily check of the puppy or dog will do a world of good. If your puppy has been playing in long grass or places where there may be thorns, pine needles, wild animals, or parasites, the check-up is a wise precaution.

Remember, regular physical examinations are tantamount to the health and long life of your dog.

SKIN DISORDERS

Apart from problems associated with lesions created by biting pests, a puppy may fall foul to a number of other skin disorders. Examples are ringworm, mange, and eczema. Ringworm is not caused by a worm, but is a fungal infection. It manifests itself as a sore-looking bald circle. If your puppy should have any form of bald patches, let your veterinarian check him over; a microscopic examination can confirm the condition. Many old remedies for ringworm exist, such as iodine, carbolic acid, formalin, and other tinctures, but modern drugs are superior.

Fungal infections can be very difficult to treat, and even more difficult to eradicate, because of the spores. These can withstand most treatments, other than burning, which is the best thing to do with bedding once the condition has been confirmed.

Mange is a general term that can be applied to many skin conditions where the hair falls out and a flaky crust develops and falls away.

Often, dogs will scratch themselves, and this invariably is worse than the original condition, for it opens lesions that are then subject to viral, fungal, or parasitic attack. The cause of the problem can be various species of mites. These either live on skin debris and the hair follicles, which they destroy, or they bury themselves just beneath the skin and feed on the tissue. Applying general remedies from pet stores is not recommended because it is essential to identify the type of mange before a specific treatment is effective.

Eczema is another non-specific term applied to many skin disorders. The condition can be brought about in many ways. Sunburn, chemicals, allergies to foods, drugs, pollens, and even stress can all produce a deterioration of the skin and coat. Given the range of causal factors, treatment can be difficult because the problem is one of identification. It is a case of taking each possibility at a time and trying to correctly diagnose the matter. If the cause is of a dietary nature then you must remove one item at a time in order to find out if the dog is allergic to a given food. It could, of course, be the lack of a nutrient that is the problem, so if the condition persists, you should consult your veterinarian.

INTERNAL DISORDERS

It cannot be overstressed that it is very foolish to attempt to diagnose an internal disorder without the advice of a veterinarian. Take a relatively common problem such as diarrhea. It might be caused by nothing more serious than the puppy hogging a lot of food or eating something that it has never previously eaten. Conversely, it could be the first indication of a potentially fatal disease. It's up to your veterinarian to make the correct diagnosis.

The following symptoms, especially if they accompany each other or are progressively added to earlier symptoms, mean you should visit the veterinarian right away:

Continual vomiting. All dogs vomit from time to time and this is not necessarily a sign of illness. They will eat grass to induce vomiting. It is a natural cleansing process common to many carnivores. However, continued vomiting is a clear sign of a problem. It may be a blockage in the pup's intestinal tract, it may be induced by worms, or it could be due to any number of diseases.

Diarrhea. This, too, may be nothing more than a temporary condition due to many factors. Even a change of home can induce diarrhea, because this often stresses the pup, and invariably there is some change in the diet. If it persists more than 48 hours then something is amiss. If blood is seen in the feces, waste no time at all in taking the dog to the vet.

Running eyes and/or nose. A pup might have a chill and this will cause the eyes and nose to weep. Again, this should quickly clear up if the puppy is placed in a warm environment and away from any drafts. If it does not, and especially if a mucous discharge is seen, then the pup has an illness that must be diagnosed.

Coughing. Prolonged coughing is a sign of a problem, usually of a respiratory nature.

Wheezing. If the pup has difficulty breathing and makes a wheezing sound when breathing, then something is wrong.

Cries when attempting to defecate or urinate. This might only be a minor problem due to the hard state of the feces, but it could be more serious, especially if the pup cries when urinating.

Cries when touched. Obviously, if you do not handle a puppy with care he might yelp. However, if he cries even when lifted gently, then he has an internal problem that becomes apparent when pressure is applied to a given area of the body. Clearly, this must be diagnosed.

Refuses food. Generally, puppies and dogs are greedy creatures when it comes to feeding time. Some might be more fussy, but none should refuse more than one meal. If they go for a number of hours without showing any interest in their food, then something is not as it should be.

General listlessness. All puppies have their off days when they do not seem their usual cheeky, mischievous selves. If this condition persists for more than two days then there is little doubt of a problem. They may not show any of the signs listed, other than perhaps a reduced interest in their food. There are many diseases that can develop internally without displaying obvious clinical signs. Blood, fecal, and other tests are needed in order to identify the disorder before it reaches an advanced state that may not be treatable.

WORMS

There are many species of worms, and a number of these live in the tissues of dogs and most other animals. Many create no problem at all, so you are not even aware they exist. Others can be tolerated in small levels, but become a major problem if they number more than a few. The most common types seen in dogs are roundworms and tapeworms. While roundworms are the greater problem, tapeworms require an intermediate host so are more easily eradicated.

Roundworms are spaghetti-like worms that cause a pot-bellied appearance and dull coat, along with more severe symptoms, such as diarrhea and vomiting. Photo courtesy of Merck AgVet.

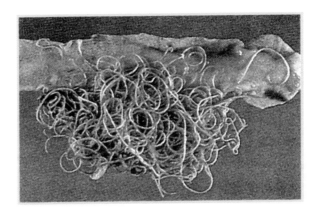

Roundworms of the species *Toxocara canis* infest the dog. They may grow to a length of 8 inches (20 cm) and look like strings of spaghetti. The worms feed on the digesting food in the pup's intestines. In chronic cases the puppy will become pot-bellied, have diarrhea, and will vomit. Eventually, he will stop eating, having passed through the stage when he always seems hungry. The worms lay eggs in the puppy and these pass out in his feces. They are then either ingested by the pup, or they are eaten by mice, rats, or beetles. These may then be eaten by the puppy and the life cycle is complete.

Larval worms can migrate to the womb of a pregnant bitch, or to her mammary glands, and this is how they pass to the puppy. The pregnant bitch can be wormed, which will help. The pups can, and should,

Whipworms are hard to find unless you strain your dog's feces, and this is best left to a veterinarian. Pictured here are adult whipworms.

be wormed when they are about two weeks old. Repeat worming every 10 to 14 days and the parasites should be removed. Worms can be extremely dangerous to young puppies, so you should be sure the pup is wormed as a matter of routine.

Tapeworms can be seen as tiny rice-like eggs sticking to the puppy's or dog's anus. They are less destructive, but still undesirable. The eggs are eaten by mice, fleas, rabbits, and other animals that serve as intermediate hosts. They develop into a larval stage and the host must be eaten by the dog in order to complete the chain. Your vet will supply a suitable remedy if tapeworms are seen or suspected. There are other worms, such as hookworms and whipworms, that are also blood suckers. They will make a pup anemic, and blood might be seen in the feces, which can be examined by the vet to confirm their presence. Cleanliness in all matters is the best preventative measure for all worms.

Heartworm infestation in dogs is passed by mosquitoes but can be prevented by a monthly (or daily) treatment that is given orally. Talk to your vet about the risk of heartworm in your area.

BLOAT (GASTRIC DILATATION)

This condition has proved fatal in many dogs, especially large and deep-chested breeds, such as the Weimaraner and the Great Dane. However, any dog can get bloat. It is caused by swallowing air during exercise, food/water gulping or another strenuous task. As many believe, it is not the result of flatulence. The stomach of an affected dog twists, disallowing food and blood flow and resulting in harmful toxins being released into the bloodstream. Death can easily follow if the condition goes undetected.

The best preventative measure is not to feed large meals or exercise your puppy or dog immediately after he has eaten. Veterinarians recommend feeding three smaller meals per day in an elevated feeding rack, adding water to dry food to prevent gulping, and not offering water during mealtimes.

VACCINATIONS

Every puppy, purebred or mixed breed, should be vaccinated against the major canine diseases. These are distemper, leptospirosis, hepatitis, and canine parvovirus. Your puppy may have received a temporary vaccination against distemper before you purchased him, but be sure to ask the breeder to be sure.

The age at which vaccinations are given can vary, but will usually be when the pup is 8 to 12 weeks old. By this time any protection given to the pup by antibodies received from his mother via her initial milk feeds will be losing their strength.

Rely on your veterinarian for the most effective vaccination schedule for your Skye Terrier puppy.

The puppy's immune system works on the basis that the white blood cells engulf and render harmless

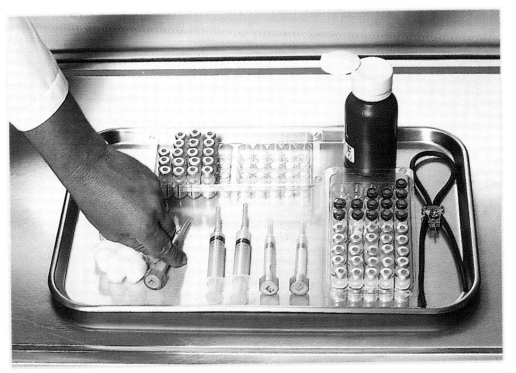

attacking bacteria. However, they must first recognize a potential enemy.

Vaccines are either dead bacteria or they are live, but in very small doses. Either type prompts the pup's defense system to attack them. When a large attack then comes (if it does), the immune system recognizes it and massive numbers of lymphocytes (white blood corpuscles) are mobilized to counter the attack. However, the ability of the cells to recognize these dangerous viruses can diminish over a period of time. It is therefore useful to provide annual reminders about the nature of the enemy. This is done by means of booster injections that keep the immune system on its alert. Immunization is not 100-percent guaranteed to be successful, but is very close. Certainly it is better than giving the puppy no protection.

Dogs are subject to other viral attacks, and if these are of a high-risk factor in your area, then your vet will suggest you have the puppy vaccinated against these as well.

Your puppy or dog should also be vaccinated against the deadly rabies virus. In fact, in many places it is illegal for your dog not to be vaccinated. This is to protect your dog, your family, and the rest of the animal population from this deadly virus that infects the nervous system and causes dementia and death.

ACCIDENTS

All puppies will get their share of bumps and bruises due to the rather energetic way they play. These will usually heal themselves over a few days. Small cuts should be bathed with a suitable disinfectant and then smeared with an antiseptic ointment. If a cut looks more serious, then stem the flow of blood with a towel or makeshift tourniquet and rush the pup to the veterinarian. Never apply so much pressure to the wound that it might restrict the flow of blood to the limb.

In the case of burns you should apply cold water or an ice pack to the surface. If the burn was due to a chemical, then this must be washed away with copious amounts of water. Apply petroleum jelly, or any vegetable oil, to the burn. Trim away the hair if need be. Wrap the dog in a blanket and rush him to the vet. The pup may go into shock, depending on the severity of the burn, and this will result in a lowered blood pressure, which is dangerous and the reason the pup must receive immediate veterinary attention.

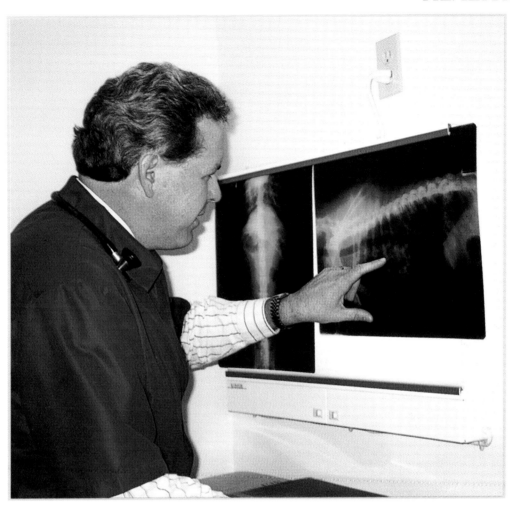

If your Skye Terrier sustains an injury from an accident or fall, acting quickly and appropriately can save his life. For example, it's a good idea to x-ray any dog hit by a car.

If a broken limb is suspected then try to keep the animal as still as possible. Wrap your pup or dog in a blanket to restrict movement and get him to the veterinarian as soon as possible. Do not move the dog's head so it is tilting backward, as this might result in blood entering the lungs.

Do not let your pup jump up and down from heights, as this can cause considerable shock to the joints. Like all youngsters, puppies do not know when enough is enough, so you must do all their thinking for them.

Provided you apply strict hygiene to all aspects of raising your puppy, and you make daily checks on his physical state, you have done as much as you can to safeguard him during his most vulnerable period. Routine visits to your veterinarian are also recommended, especially while the puppy is under one year of age. The vet may notice something that did not seem important to you.

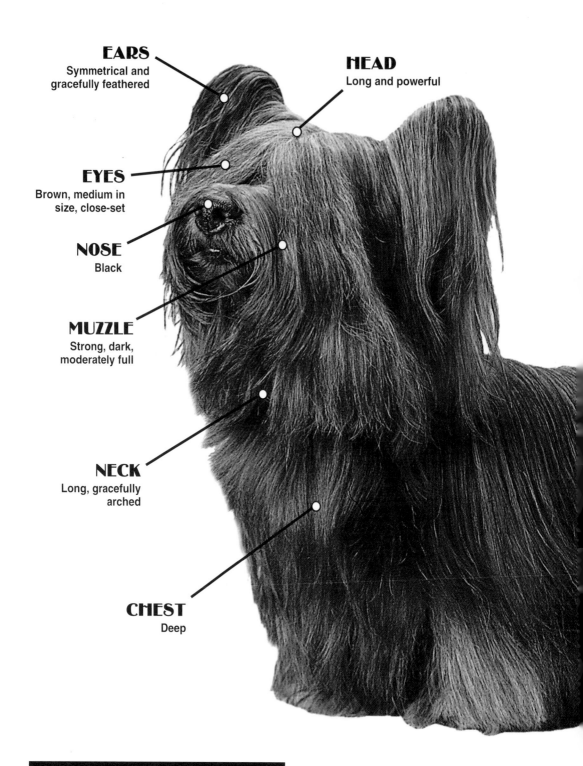

EARS
Symmetrical and
gracefully feathered

HEAD
Long and powerful

EYES
Brown, medium in
size, close-set

NOSE
Black

MUZZLE
Strong, dark,
moderately full

NECK
Long, gracefully
arched

CHEST
Deep

Westminster Kennel Club 1997 Best of Breed
winner Ch. Longwood Piper's Promise, owned
by Wayne R. Herman.